Pricing Without Fear

A Sewing Entrepreneur's Guide

by
Barbara Wright Sykes

Featuring

Saundra Weed	Susan Khalje
Bonnie L. Motts	Jane Ambrose
Trenia Bell-Will	Fred Bloebaum

COLLINS PUBLICATIONS
Chino Hills, CA 91709

Pricing Without Fear

A Sewing Entrepreneurs Guide
by
Barbara Wright Sykes

PUBLISHED BY:
COLLINS PUBLICATIONS
3233 GRAND AVENUE, SUITE N-294
Chino Hills, CA 91709

Cover Design by: Ann Collins
Layout and Design: Ann Collins

Edited by:
Gail Taylor Walton
Stephanie Rupp
Nancy Aldredge

LCCN: 99-075012
ISBN: 0-9632857-6-9

Table Of Contents

** *Represents Illustrations or Charts*

Disclaimer

There are pros and cons to be argued when it comes to selecting a pricing method that is best for your business. When considering a pricing method, do not compare your business with that of someone else. There are a number of variables to be considered; for example, the fact that a sewing professional may choose to operate *their* business out of a commercial location rather than their home. This could influence *their* pricing greatly. Keep in mind that your goals and objectives may be entirely different from your colleagues'. Therefore, it may *not* be in your best interest to price your goods and services by the same methods.

In this book you will examine many pricing methods by noted sewing professionals. Select a method that works best for your business. No matter what pricing method you select for your business, the publisher and author of this book, and the featured sewing authorities, cannot guarantee the success or profitability of any one given pricing method. Therefore, selecting a method from this book should be done at your discretion.

Introduction

Why A Book On Pricing?

Pricing without fear should be second nature…but it is not. What I have found is that of all the concerns sewing professionals have, pricing seems to be number one. My motivation for writing this book was to reassure sewing professionals that they can have a healthy business, and not be afraid to price for profit. I had to ask myself if I had ever been afraid to price my goods and services. Looking back, I must say that I have never experienced fear with respect to pricing. I have always been confident in my ability to price for profit. There are strong reasons why I haven't feared pricing for profit; it stems from the fact that I majored in business and understood the psychology of pricing. I think having this knowledge helped to eliminate any fear I may have experienced otherwise.

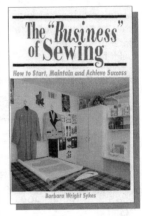

When I penned *The "Business" Of Sewing,* I covered the basic pricing methods, and gave illustrations. I briefly addressed overcoming doubt, fear and procrastination, which I later devoted a whole book to. Once I became more aware of how many people suffered from the fear of pricing, I recorded an audio entitled, *Take The Fear Out Of Pricing,* complete with exercises and worksheets.

When I am on the lecture circuit my most requested seminar is on pricing. Consequently, I decided to dedicate a whole book to overcoming the fear of pricing. I had just about completed the book when I realized that it would be a good idea to have other sewing professionals share their views as well. Thus, I invited several of the industry's leading authorities to offer their perspectives. I am pleased to introduce my esteemed colleagues: Saundra Weed, Trenia Bell-Will, Susan Khalje, Bonnie L. Motts, Jane Ambrose and Fred Bloebaum.

Featured Guests

Saundra Weed is the author of *Creative Sewing As A Business*. Ms. Weed designs wearable art and jewelry, and specializes in the restoration and restyling of vintage wedding gowns and is the owner of *Artistic Images*. Her sewing and "how-to" articles appear regularly in such national publications as *Wearable Crafts* magazine. Ms. Weed is the guru of pricing for creative sewing. If you have questions about her seminars or want to purchase Saundra Weed's books, please contact her at Artistic Images, 30784 Grandview, Westland, MI 48186 or by phone: 734-728-2535.

Trenia Bell-Will is a successful independent pattern designer and owner of the *Interiors Institute*. Some of her original custom designs have been published by the *McCall Pattern Company* and featured in their catalogs. She specializes in interior design and has a wealth of talent. Trenia is an excellent instructor in the field of interior design and a leader in developing construction techniques for sewing custom interiors. If you have questions about Trenia's seminars and patterns, please contact her at Trenia Bell-Will's Interiors Institute, 904 Dundee Drive, Radford, VA 24141 or bellwill@aol.com.

Susan Khalje is the author of *Bridal Couture, Linen and Cotton: Classic Sewing Techniques for Great Results*, and a featured writer for *Threads*, *Sew News*, and *Vogue Patterns Magazine*. Susan is a consummate instructor; she founded the Bridal Sewing School (now *The Couture Sewing School*) in 1993. As a designer, Susan's gowns are priceless. Susan was also the former chair for the Professional Association of Custom Clothiers. If you want more information on her seminars and books, please contact her at The Couture Sewing School, 4600 Breidenbaugh Lane, Glenarm, MD 21057, or call: 410-592-5711, FAX: 410-592-6913

Bonnie L. Motts is a couture designer and dressmaker, and owner of *Bon's Place "Your Total Image Studio."* She is also a professional image consultant, fashion coordinator, skin care specialist, and make-up artist, to men, women, and teens providing the *Total Image Solution*. Bonnie offers training, workbooks, worksheets, and BeautiControl skin care and cosmetic products. If you want more information on her customized sewing, image seminars, and training materials, please contact Bonnie at Bon's Place "Your Total Image Studio", 5440 Frank Road NW, North Canton, Ohio 44720, or call: 330-499-3346, Fax: 330-499-4827 or mottsbon@aol.

Jane Ambrose (Button) is the author of *Consultant-in-a-Box: A Practical, Hands-On, How-To-Guide for Operating, Building & Creating Your Own Apparel or Knitting Business; Guide to Starting a Clothing Company* and *Knitter's Guide to Starting a Business*. She is a business consultant specializing in creative product development, production, merchandising a line, pricing, costing, sales and marketing. Jane started Warm Heart, a wholesale apparel business, which grew into a national brand name. She recently launched her own pattern line—Warm Heart Patterns, featuring children's coordinated clothing. For more information about Jane's seminars, consulting, books or patterns, please contact her at 360-856-5224, email button@wytbear.com or write 1039 Sterling Road, Sedro-Woolley, WA 98284.

Fred Bloebaum ("Fred" short for La Fred—a woman with a man's nickname) launched the release of her own line of patterns, *"Clothing Designs by La Fred."* Her patterns provide elegant, classic clothing that have contemporary lines and are easy to construct. Fred is a regular instructor at *The Sewing Workshop,* and teaches workshops at conferences and fabric stores around the country. She is also a contributor to *Threads* magazine. Fred's specialties include tailoring; sewing with specialty fabrics; figure analysis and wardrobe selection; and interpreting fine designer sewing techniques.. She is also a member of The Professional Association of Custom Clothiers. To obtain more information regarding her patterns, you may call: 510-893-6811.

As the author of *Pricing Without Fear*, it gives me great pleasure to feature Saundra Weed, Trenia Bell-Will, Susan Khalje, Bonnie L. Motts, Jane Ambrose and Fred Bloebaum. A brilliant collection of pricing savvy and wisdom can be found in the experiences of these experts. It doesn't matter whether you specialize in bridal, home décor, custom tailoring, wearable art, alterations, sewing for children, or making crafts; you will benefit and enjoy reading about their secrets to success. These dynamic individuals bring enormous knowledge and expertise, making *Pricing Without Fear* a wonderful tool to eliminate your fears.

Get Your Questions Answered

For questions regarding *Pricing Without Fear,* or want to send questions to the featured guests for Collins Publications *Sewing For Profit Forum* on our web site www.collinspub.com, you may email them to: sewing@collinspub.com, or send your questions to:

Collins Publications
3233 Grand Avenue, Suite N-294C
Chino Hills, CA 91709

Let's get started!   *Let's get started!*

Are You Afraid Of Pricing?

The Value Principle

Pricing seems to give everyone heartburn. They fear whether they will be effective at pricing their goods and services in the marketplace in order to earn a profit. Why does pricing create such fear? First and foremost, many individuals simply do not understand the psychology behind pricing. Some feel that they aren't qualified to be paid what they are worth; while others throw caution to the wind when it comes to affixing the right pricing structure to a service and product based business.

There are several approaches to pricing that merit discussion. First, you must not be misled by the belief that pricing is based solely on math alone. Yes, there are definitely mathematical formulas that must be applied in order to price your goods and services. However, garnering a profit and continuing to sustain that profit margin goes far beyond establishing a price.

How can you get more for your goods and services? Why do consumers buy goods and services? What motivates them to part with their discretionary dollars? Careful research of consumer behavior will uncover the answers to these questions. You must understand that consumers respond out of need, want and desire. Consumers spend because of value. That's what separates the K-Mart Shopper from the Nordstrom shopper—it's called value.

People pay for value, whether real or perceived. You can create the concept of value through offering excellent service, convenience, packaging, and having goods or services that satisfy the wants, needs and desires of the ultimate consumer. You must educate the consumer and let them know you exist; this process is achieved through proper marketing, advertising and promotions. Pointing out the utilitarian value, convenience or service that will be derived from the purchase of your goods and services is the key.

Consumers spend because of aesthetic value—packaging. Is it attractive? Does having the product or doing business with you enhance the social position of the consumer? If they can see the value in doing business with you, they will be more inclined to make that almighty purchasing decision. Don't forget that people are image conscious and will spend to cultivate and maintain their image, even if it means paying a little more.

People also place a great deal of importance on their time. The issue of convenience generally means saving time; and as we all know, time is money. The thought process follows that I may pay a little more for the convenience; however, it will save me in the long run. Thus, value is further demonstrated.

The elements of consumer behavior are paramount to the pricing of a product or service. The aforementioned elements are the key issues that help to build what is called demand. When you have consumer demand for your goods and services, it gives you the fuel needed to charge a higher price. However, you must consider your competition. In order to protect your share of the marketplace you must become innovative in your business and offer something that will distinguish you from your competition. It could be in the form of extended hours, better customer service, free gift wrapping, waiving the first hour of consultation if they book several with you, and so on.

Finally, the actual calculation of the bottom line—the price, must be considered. There are certain pricing structures that are better suited for a service based business rather than a product based business, and in certain businesses a combination of pricing structures should be applied. Let's examine the three basic pricing structures: (1) The flat fee, (2) by the hour and (3) the integrated pricing structure.

Are You Afraid Of Pricing?

A large number of sewing professionals experience anxiety from the fear of pricing. They will make every excuse in the book regarding why no one will pay "them" what they are worth. The following is a compilation of questions, comments and concerns issued by sewing entrepreneurs.

- "What is the *standard* price I should charge?"
- "My family won't pay me for my services."
- "I don't charge my family!"
- "I am intimidated by what others are charging for their services."
- "I feel you must give your friends and family discounts."
- "I am afraid to ask to be paid upon completion of the project."
- "I feel guilty when it's time to get paid for a project."
- "I don't know how to calculate labor or production on a project."
- "I fear my customers will say: 'You are too expensive. Mary doesn't charge that much!'"
- "I don't need to market my sewing, my family, friends and neighbors like my work."
- "Advertising is only for big companies."
- "I don't charge that much because I work out of my home."
- "I don't charge my clients for shopping."
- "I don't charge to sew on buttons, they're so small."
- "I couldn't charge for that!"
- "I do this part-time so I don't charge that much."
- "I live in a geographical location where people just won't pay "that" much for my services."
- "She's so nice I feel guilty charging her that much."

If you have ever made any one of these comments or even thought about it, then you definitely have a fear of pricing, or perhaps you may not fully understand how to price for profit. Our goal is to eliminate those fears, give you solid information, and show you how to price for profit. Before we get into the various pricing methods, let's look at some of the concerns sewing entrepreneurs experience.

Examining Your Fears

"What is the standard price you should charge?"

There is no "standard" price that should be charged for your goods and services. It is predicated upon two elements: The Proprietary Factor and the Consumer Factor. You should consider both the proprietary as well as the consumer factors when pricing for profit.

Proprietary Factor: It is called the proprietary factor because it deals with issues that are of concern to the business owner, or proprietor. As a sewing entrepreneur you are concerned with overhead expenses, your desired salary or gross profit, and the hours that will be committed to your business in order to make it profitable. These factors, and many others are taken into consideration along with those of the consumers.

Consumer Factor: Consumer buying habits are influenced by a great number of things. When doing business with sewing entrepreneurs, consumers are preoccupied with the quality of your goods and services, as well as your knowledge and expertise in the field. Above all, there has to be a demand on the part of the consumer for your goods and service before they will depart with that almighty dollar. These are just a few of the issues that you should consider when thinking about consumer behavior. For a more comprehensive listing see *"Factors That Influence Consumer Spending."*

"My family won't pay me for my services." Or you say: "I don't charge my family!"
And you say: " I feel I must give my friends and family a discounts."

Let's get this straight, "Are you in business to earn a profit, or are you in business to win friends and influence people?" If you picked the first one, then you must adjust your thinking regarding working for family and friends. First of all you don't want to work for *anyone* who does not respect your business, especially family and friends. This is not a hobby for you and you can't treat it like a hobby, charging some while giving your services away to others. No one will respect you, and least of all your business. It is your job to set the stage for a healthy working relationship in your business, and that process starts when you change your attitude about your business. Your family members are no doubt wonderful people. However, no one else in business will give them anything free because they happen to be "your family and friends," so why would you? This may sound harsh or somewhat selfish, but I can guarantee you that many a sewing business has fallen by the wayside due to family and friends taking advantage of the sewing entrepreneur. This is not to say that you cannot extend a courtesy discount, but be sure it is one you can live with, and one that doesn't drain the profits from your business.

"I am intimidated by what other people are charging for their sewing services."

I couldn't believe my ears when I first heard a novice sewing professional say that. I quickly explained to her that her worth as a sewing professional should not be predicated upon what others are charging. Did it ever occur to her that they could be doing it all wrong? It doesn't matter if they are charging more or less than she is, she is pricing her goods and services properly. You should never be intimidated by someone else's ability to price higher fees or feel that you are overcharging if your pricing structure happens to be higher than someone else's. If you have taken into consideration the proprietary and consumer factors when designing your pricing and you are getting the desired results, that is all that matters.

"I feel guilty asking to get paid for a project, and I am afraid to ask for money upon completion of the project."

You should only feel guilty about getting paid if you have not done your best on the project; you didn't complete the project in a timely manner, or you didn't follow the client's wishes according to the contract agreement . There should be no other reason for you to feel guilty about getting paid for services rendered. You agreed to perform the services on the contract and the client agreed to pay. Below is a quote from my book, *The "Business" Of Sewing*, which I feel drives the point home.

"When the client arrives to pickup the garment, make sure she is completely satisfied before you present the invoice. If the client is pleased with the project and has no objections, you may introduce the invoice for final payment. At this point, you should feel very confident in asking the client for final payment on the project. You have successfully performed a service and your client is happy, now you will be rewarded for having done so. Remember to exude confidence and keep a pleasant expression as you reach for your receipt book! By now you should be comfortable saying, 'Will that be cash, or would you prefer to write a check?'" My business has progressed to the point that I now offer my clients the convenient use of credit cards. I smile as I reach for the receipt book and I simply say, " Will that be cash, check or charge?"

"I don't know how to calculate labor or production on a project."

Reading resources to help you understand pricing and the various pricing methods will give you insight into how to price for profit. Understanding consumer behavior and their buying patterns, as well as knowing your own personal wants, needs and desires in your business will help shape and mold your pricing decisions. Be sure to gain a thorough knowledge of marketing, as this will help you to capture the attention of the ultimate consumer. It does you absolutely no good to have the best pricing structure and no one knows you exist. There is a resource worth mentioning entitled *Marketing Your Sewing Business*. This is an audio tape complete with worksheets and exercises to help you understand the marketing process with respect to a sewing business. Another excellent book is *Secrets To Personal Marketing Power*. See order form at the end of this text.

"I fear customers will make comparisons by saying: "You are too expensive. Mary doesn't charge that much!"

My first thought upon hearing someone make this statement was, you should want them to go to Mary; obviously they have no frame of reference when it comes to hiring a true professional. A true professional is one who will provide quality service and complete their projects in a timely manner. They invest time and effort into elevating their knowledge and skill level in order to provide the best workmanship and service available. They value their business and are not so desperate that they are inclined to give away their services. If your client makes this statement, it is possible that you may not have educated him or her on how valuable your services are to them. Part of price resistance is due to lack of knowledge. Our job is to educate the client on our business, our goods and services and what they can expect from us, and what we expect from them. The use of a *Client Call Sheet* will help you evaluate each prospect prior to the first face-to-face interview. You will decide if you want to work with them and you will educate them at the same time. I assure you that after careful screening of all clients who show up at your doorstep for projects, you will eliminate price resistance. You will have conveyed your value and determined that they are worthy of your services, thus you get paid what you are worth! Note: Client Call Sheet comes in the Complete Set Of Forms and Forms On Computer Disk. See order form at the end of this book.

"I don't need to market my sewing business, my family, friends and neighbors like my work."

Huge mistake! Never rely solely on your family, friends and neighbors to completely support your business. It is too small a sphere of influence to run a business on. There is too much emotion tied up in decision making, and far too narrow a market to earn a profit. For most sewing entrepreneurs, it is too delicate a relationship and they tend to lose perspective when it comes to the health and profitability of their business. Enter family and friends, out goes profit. You have to have the stomach for handling clients when there is personal feeling involved, and truthfully, not many people have the knack for it, not to mention depending on that kind of a relationship to earn a living. Nine times out of ten, most of your profit winds up being absorbed into what is called family discounts! They feel that the relationship gives them the right to rob you of your profit margin, although they won't say it. Final thoughts on this philosophy: *Market, Market, Market!* Enough said!

"Advertising is only for big companies."

Let's examine this statement for a minute. How in the world did "big" companies get to be "big"? How about *Marketing*, *Advertising* and *Promotions*. Ever hear of that? I rest my case.

Get Your Questions Answered

For questions regarding *Pricing Without Fear*, or you want to send questions to the featured guests for Collins Publications *Sewing For Profit Forum* on our web site www.collinspub.com, you may email them to: sewing@collinspub.com, or send your questions to:

Collins Publications ◆ 3233 Grand Avenue, Suite N-294C ◆ Chino Hills, CA 91709

Not Ready For Prime Time!

The following are statements made by people who want to run a hobby not a business:
   "I couldn't charge for that!"
   "I don't charge my clients for shopping."
   "I do this part-time, so I don't charge that much."
   "She's so nice I feel guilty charging her that much."
   "I don't charge to sew on buttons, they're so small."
   "I don't charge that much because I work out of my home."

Geographical Paranoia

"I live in a geographical location where people just won't pay "that" much for my services."
   I cannot tell you how many times I have heard this excuse; I cringe every time I hear it. The irony lies in the fact that some sewing professionals really believe that the only business available is that which is within their small sphere of influence—family, friends, neighbors and people living in their community. I always say, "If my business was solely dependent on my geographical location, I would be out of business!"
   Entrepreneurs can't become geographically complacent. No business will grow from planting one seed. You must be open to the possibility that seeds can germinate in different soil. For instance, you can advertise your business in your community, and in other communities where they have consumers with discretionary income to support your business. There is nothing to say that you are limited by your present location. Your job is to know your customers' social and economic profile, and how to capture their attention so that they will do business with you. I can tell you from experience that they are not all going to live in your community.
   Just think about it for a minute, corporations and companies that have become a household name didn't do so by just planting a seed in one geographical location. They were open to a broad base of business opportunities and were innovative in how to make them work. As sewing professionals, we too have many possibilities to make our businesses work. Let's examine some of them. Instead of the customer coming to you, perhaps you can go to the customer and charge mileage for offering the service of convenience. Or, maybe you will make items and sell them through mail order. With technology being so sophisticated, we have the ability to typeset and print out our own color brochures, complete with logos, graphics and pictures. If you structure your marketing, advertising and promotions to demonstrate your value, customers will come to you from miles around. I have had the pleasure of securing customers as far as 50 to 100 miles from my geographical location. The objective of my promotional campaign was to convey why it was important to do business with me, and why I would be of value to the ultimate consumer. If you plant the seeds properly you will get the clientele that will pay you what you are worth, and will go to great lengths to do so.
   Before we examine factors that influence consumers to buy, let me throw out one more thing for you to consider: Have you ever thought about networking with other qualified sewing professionals? Periodically my fellow sewing associates and I will exchange services. For example, I specialize in custom tailoring and my colleague specializes in bridal. I might have a client in her community that I can't go to (at that time) who needs to be measured, etc. My colleague will take the measurements and perform certain clerical functions pertinent to the contract and forward that information to me. I will either return the favor or give her a service fee. Thus, I am able to do business out of my geographical location. A word of caution, if you are going to exercise this method, be sure your colleague has the proper knowledge and expertise to perform the needed services. Our goal is to become successful sewing professionals, therefore we can't entertain geographical paranoia!

Factors That Influence Consumer Spending

Understanding Consumer Behavior

    Sewing for profit can be extremely rewarding, both financially and from the sheer joy that it brings. However, it will never bring you the personal satisfaction you deserve if you do not know how to properly price your goods and services. There are many elements to pricing for profit. It goes deeper than just mathematical calculations, or copying someone else's pricing structure. Let's examine some of the elements involved in pricing, and those that directly influence the consumers desire to spend.

Factors That Influence Consumer Spending	
Quality	Convenience
Wants	Obsolescence
Needs	Seasons
Desires	Style
Price	Society/Peer Pressure
Trends	Economy
Brand Awareness	Product Reliability
Word of Mouth	Sales
Discounts/Coupons	Service
Method of Payment	Established Relationships
Image	Variety
One Stop Shopping	Knowledge/Expertise
Comfortable Environment	Sales Staff/Entrepreneur
Reputation	Marketing/Advertising/Promotions
Distribution	E-Commerce
Demand	Disposable Income

Quality and Product Reliability: Two words readily come to mind when thinking about product—reliability and durability. In speaking about quality, consumers are more inclined to buy a product or service if the quality is excellent. This is not a new phenomenon, but one that some entrepreneurs tend to forget. You have heard the old saying: "You get what you pay for." People will pay more for good quality. It is called value. If quality and product reliability are present, the consumer can easily see the value in doing business with you, and they don't mind paying for it. Because of the value principle, some people prefer to shop at Nordstrom where the skies the limit.

Knowledge and Expertise: One of fastest ways to become obsolete in the marketplace is to fail to keep your knowledge and expertise current. Your clients come to you because you are the expert, and they are willing to pay you for your knowledge and expertise. In a business where you provide a service or consultation, such as a sewing business, your knowledge and expertise regarding your field of specialty is more apparent. Working in close contact with the client makes it easier to sense whether you know what you are doing. Customer confidence and their willingness to pay you what you are worth requires that you maintain your knowledge and skill level at all times.

Wants, Needs and Desires: The three basic reasons why consumers buy are wants, needs and desires. Your job as a sewing professional is to understand each. More importantly, you must understand what goods and services you have that will satiate the wants, needs and desires of the ultimate consumer. Next, you must know how to capture their attention, so that they will depart with some of those disposable or discretionary dollars and do business with you.

What can you do to influence your customers to come back—again, and again, and again?

Demand: In economics there is a philosophy called supply and demand. When a good or service is in short supply, and the demand for it is high, the price goes up. Let's say that a large corporation relocated their executives to your town and built homes for them. You are an expert in home décor and you live in a rural community where there aren't any interior decorators and few department stores that cater to the needs of the homeowner with respect to home décor. With the influx of the new homeowners and the need for your talents, coupled with the lack of adequate supply of services for their needs, it is safe to say that you are in demand. According to the law of supply and demand you are king when it comes to your pricing and getting the business.

Service: It is not enough to have an excellent product if you can't extend the one thing that seems to be overlooked, especially in our microwave society, and that is service. You have heard consumers say: "I shop there because the service is better." This element of consumer buying has never changed. It ranks right up there with quality, reliability and durability. Consumers want to receive good service, and they want the sewing professional to be just that—a professional.

Established Relationships, Sales Staff and the Entrepreneur: Customers often continue to frequent a business because they like the salesperson or the waitress or consultant. They have formed a healthy rapport with this individual and like the relationship that has developed. It makes them comfortable and secure. Customers will drive out of their way to take their business to a place where they have established a relationship. The key ingredient to establishing a good relationship with the consumer lies in the hands of the sales staff and the owner of the business. It is the job of the owner to define how the consumer is to be treated by making storewide policies regarding the service the customer should receive. The owner should always seek customer comments to determine if the level of service is meeting the needs of the ultimate consumer.

Word Of Mouth, Reputation, and Image: Service plus quality equals your reputation. What additional factors build strong image and reputation? Your ability to operate your business as a business not a hobby. Caring enough to dress professionally, completing clients projects in a timely manner, paying attention to details, and the fact that you genuinely care about the well-being of your clients. This is what creates your image, forms a good reputation and translates into word-of-mouth recommendations regarding your business. There can be no dollar value placed upon customer loyalty garnered by a good reputation and positive business image.

Price: Price is important to certain segments of the population. Your job is to determine where the level of price resistance is. However, keeping in mind that you cannot satisfy everyone, and you are establishing your prices with a specific clientele in mind—those who can afford it! Thus, you will structure your price list and your marketing efforts to attract those clients, and you will refuse to entertain those who say you are too high.

Method of Payment: We are living in a plastic society. Virtually everyone has at least one credit card, some have so many they could qualify as collectors. When I decided to offer the use of credit cards in my business, I was astounded at how much it actually increased my profit margin. One of my very best clients said to me: "I am so glad that you accept credit cards, now I can spend more money with you!" And spend, she did. That is the best testimony I can give for the argument to offer the leading credit cards.

Coupons and Discounts: Some consumers tend to respond to these offers. However, this method of attracting consumer attention should not be overused. It should be utilized periodically, but not to the extent that you become known as a bargain-basement sewing professional.

Trends: There is a large segment of the population that follows trends, no matter whether they are trends in fashion, or trends in home décor. Keeping abreast of these trends can help you appeal to that segment and allow you to further increase your profit margin.

Style: In my experience as a sewing professional, I have identified my clients who are extremely conscious of their own personal style. These are my clients who will pay for their clothing to be made at all cost. They don't want to be duplicated; they are not trend followers. They are dissatisfied with department stores because they are limited in selection with respect to fabric, color, silhouette and design. Therefore, they seek out my services for custom tailoring. With these options available, they feel empowered, and that is valuable to them. So I capitalize on this concept in my marketing. I market to this segment of the population: the more affluent corporate executive, with lots of disposable income where money is no object. This allows me to charge higher prices because I fully understand the wants, needs and desires of my customer.

Seasons: Just as we have certain seasons of the year, there are certain goods and services that are seasonal. Planning your marketing efforts around this philosophy will give you the competitive edge. You must be careful to fill off-peak and off-season with other goods and services that can help you maintain a profit in the interim.

Society and Peer Pressure: Also known as, "keeping up with the Jones's." Throughout history man has striven to keep up with his neighbors, colleagues, family, friends, peers and society standards. Why? The answer lies in the fact that the drive is so strong to fit in; to be in the rank and file, and to be a part of the status quo. It compels us to spend money we don't even have. We want to "be, do and have" what others in society possess. Some people follow trends as though they were gospel.

Obsolescence: In my marketing classes, I learned that some manufacturers make products with obsolescence in mind. It works in their favor because it gives the consumer a need to repeatedly do business with them. For instance, let's say you are a manufacturer of eight-track tapes. Now, when you first planned the eight-track tape you also planned the cassette tape. Your strategy was to introduce the eight tracks, and entice all the major manufacturers of electronic stereo devices to offer them in their units. Furthermore, you had set a specific time frame for the life cycle of the eight-track. It would last three years prior to the introduction of the cassette tape, with eventual phase out of the eight tracks, making the eight tracks become completely obsolete. Your job is to watch the market and offer products that satisfy obsolescence. Perhaps in your business you will have a product life cycle with a replacement in mind. The computer industry is notorious for doing this. Where is the 286 CPU? Or the first floppy disk? Did someone mention DVD?

Brand Awareness: Some consumers buy, not because the product has been tried and proven effective—at least not by them. They buy because they have been made aware of that brand. We are programmed through repetitious, subliminal advertising. A customer could be standing in the middle of the aisle pondering a bath soap purchase, never having tried any of the available brands on the shelf: he or she will purchase the one with the most famous brand recognition. Consumer philosophy chants: "I've heard of it, so it must be good!"

Economy and Disposable Income: In a stable economy where the dollar is strong, interest rates are low, unemployment is down; and consumer confidence tends to be high. Not to mention that consumers have more disposable income and are eager to part with it. You find purchases of clothing and household articles at an all-time high. These are times where you are least likely to experience price resistance. People feel less intimidated in spending on leisure and luxury items. This could represent a prime opportunity for you to market and capture the attention of the more affluent consumer.

One Stop Shopping and Variety: As a business consultant, I have had the pleasure of working with a number of sewing professionals. One client in particular stands out in my mind. She owned a bridal shop and wanted to increase her profit margin by a certain percentage. When she hired me she had never heard of the concept of *in-kind* businesses. In-kind businesses can help to raise profit levels. Consumers are very busy people and they prefer to shop where they can acquire a number of products and services all at once. It saves time, money and stress. They like the idea of a one stop shopping experience. In the case of my client, she made items for the bride, mother-of-bride, etc. However, she didn't offer much in the way other products: cake, invitations, photography, limousine, tuxedo rental, etc. What we did was negotiate contracts with these in-kind businesses, bringing samples, photo albums, etc., into her bridal shop, therefore making my client a one-stop shopping opportunity for the bridal party. Within the first quarter of implementation she increased her profit margin by 50%. What was so appealing to the bridal party was that my client had a variety of products to choose from in each category, further making the entire experience a sheer joy.

Comfortable Environment: I had a client once who told me—in the middle of a fitting—that she enjoys doing business with me because my office and my sewing studio were so comfortable. She liked the décor, lighting and the privacy. I operate my custom tailoring business out of my home. She said that there are some places that make her uncomfortable, and she refuses to shop there no matter how good the price may be. In fact, she shared that when she was in Cleveland she had gone to a sewing professional who had been recommended to her because she was so reasonable (cheap). She had gone there with high expectations. The lady came to the door dressed like a bag lady… the place was a wreck! It was early in the afternoon and the lady had her children running around unsupervised. My client said she didn't care how reasonable the lady was, she wanted her shopping experience to feel good. She stated that she didn't book the project and never returned to do business with her.

Convenience: Customers adore convenience. Convenience comes in many ways: location, method of payment, one-stop shopping, hours and days of business, and variety of products and services. Think of ways you can make the shopping experience convenient for your customers and capitalize on it. It could be the one ingredient that sets you apart from your competition.

Distribution: This applies mainly to businesses where they rely upon others to make their products available to the public. If you rely upon this form of doing business, it is imperative that your distribution channels be in place prior to starting any marketing, advertising or promotions campaign. If you are selling wholesale, distribution could be a key factor in positioning your products in the marketplace. You could lose clients by advertising that products are sold and available, when in essence they are not available due to poor distribution efforts.

E-Commerce: I never thought I would be able to sit at home and do all my shopping from a computer. The Internet has opened a whole new shopping and business experience. However, in a sewing business I still prefer to have face-to-face contact with my clients. There is something surreal about making a project for someone whom you have never fitted or personally taken measurements for. I am not saying it can't be done. I have worked with my colleagues to take measurements of my clients who live in other geographical locations. As a business consultant, I have clients that do it all the time and love not having the client present. In defense of this new wave of business, it does work. A web presence is absolutely necessary to participate in e-commerce. Consumer confidence has risen and people are less fearful of placing orders on the Internet which require leaving credit card information. When I attended a Tech-Net meeting at Microsoft last November, one of the consultants said that eventually we will not have to leave our homes for anything. We can shop through e-commerce and even find a mate and get married all on the Internet. I guess anything is possible since we can now do our banking and have our clothes cleaned from a grocery store. The possibilities are endless!

Marketing, Advertising and Promotions: I can't help but say it again: How in the world did "big" companies get to be "big?" How about "Marketing, Advertising and Promotions?" A well thought out and executed plan can put your goods and services before the attention of millions of consumers. It can influence what they think and how they think about you and your goods and service. It can change a "want" into a need. The right campaign can create demand. With some degree of planning and market manipulation you can force the price to increase. Case in point: Elmo, Cabbage Patch, Furbies, and Beanie Babies, are just a few products that have enjoyed price increase and market demand as a result of a brilliant promotional campaign. Brand and product awareness are also spawned through the use of a strategic campaign. There are two types of methods to consider when planning your marketing, advertising and promotional campaign; traditional and non-traditional. The latter is more cost effective. *Marketing Your Sewing Business Audio* and *The "Business" Of Sewing* cover these subjects in more detail. * To order these audios, see the order form at the end of this book.

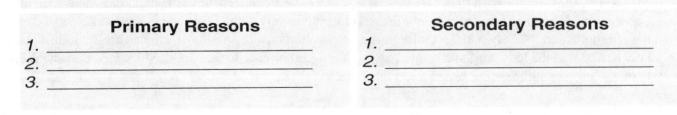

Do You Know Your Customers?

From the chart "Factors That Influence Consumer Spending," list six reasons why customers would do business with you. List primary and secondary ones.

Primary Reasons

1. _____
2. _____
3. _____

Secondary Reasons

1. _____
2. _____
3. _____

The History of Pricing

Why do we need to consider pricing? In the old days, and even today, some people practice the art of bartering. Bartering is trading one good or service in exchange for another. In this type of transaction, generally there is no money transferred between parties. One drawback to this method of exchange is determining equal value. One good or service may not carry the same weight or exchange value. Consequently, one of the parties to the transaction loses. He or she has now traded their goods and services for lesser value. One of the other concerns lies in the fact that not all things can be acquired through bartering; and currency and coins are still required to purchase certain goods and services. Bartering is not a monetary yield system, thus leaving you with no method by which you can purchase traditional goods and services.

Realizing that bartering had its drawbacks, a method of exchange had to be established so that we could purchase items at fair market value. The medium of exchange happened to be called money. Money was assigned a weight, or value. To determine what an item should cost, it was assigned a value in proportion with the weight of the currency and coins, better known as money.

Now that a medium of exchange was established, the next hurdle was to assign goods and services a value or price. The assumption was that the price would represent even exchange; you give "X" amount of money for "X" amount of goods and services. Sounds easy? The majority of sewing professionals would disagree. It is a well known fact that pricing for profit tends to be one of the most stressful ordeals for most entrepreneurs.

The stress comes from not knowing if they have priced too high or too low, or if they have selected the proper pricing strategy for their business. Some arbitrarily assign value based upon their instincts, and many have preconceived ideas about what they are worth, without giving any respect to the elements involved in pricing. More often than not, they tend to undervalue their goods and services. Ultimately, in due time, the business suffers and the entrepreneur folds.

To relieve your fears, it should be noted that there is no hidden agenda or secret society that successful entrepreneurs belong to. The bottom line is that you must understand how to price effectively. Plan, do and review your pricing structure to ensure its effectiveness.

Why Review A Profitable Pricing Method?

As consumer needs shift and develop, it will affect how they do business with you. Technology will also play a major role in your pricing. Your ability to complete projects, and the time it takes you to do so will affect pricing as well. The increase or decrease of clients will influence whether or not you need to hire employees or subcontract out projects. The fact that you may have outgrown your present location due to increased clientele will affect your pricing too. As you can see, there are a myriad of concerns that could affect pricing. If you know how to price and how to monitor your pricing policy, it will keep your business healthy.

Pricing Methods 101

Bartering was not a perfect system for obtaining goods and services. It was clear that a monetary means of exchange had to be embraced; and a method needed to be developed to do so. The two most popular forms of determining value were the *Flat Fee* and *By The Hour* methods. It wasn't until sometime later with the advent of service and product based businesses that the *Integrated Pricing Method* was introduced. well as a number of other pricing methods.

The Bottom Line On Pricing

There are pros and cons to be argued when it comes to selecting a pricing method that is best for your business. When considering a pricing method, do not compare your business with that of someone else. There are a number of variables to be considered. For example, the fact that you operate your business out of your home rather than a commercial location will influence *your* pricing. Keep in mind that your goals and objectives may be entirely different from your colleagues'. Therefore, it may not be in your best interest to price your goods and services by the same methods. In this book you will examine many pricing methods by noted sewing professionals. Select a method that works best for your business. No matter what pricing method you select for your business, you must consider the following:

1. Your production time
2. Your overhead expenses
3. Direct expenses
4. The hours you will commit to your business
5. The socioeconomic profile of your customer

Flat Fee Method

Marge M.

December 10th at exactly 4 PM, Marge turned off her sewing machine, sat in her chair, looked around the room and burst into tears. Marge had been up all night working on a project. She was literally exhausted and saw very little progress. She had been in business for six months and had an inordinate number of clients--a situation most sewing professionals would kill for.

The customer had an appointment with Marge the next day to pick up her project, and Marge had at least three quarters left to complete—with no help in sight. The project itself was not that difficult, however, Marge's pricing method left no room for the intense labor design details requested by the customer. Her pricing policy was predicated upon the flat fee method. Marge had been making these items in mass and selling them to customers at a set price. When she started her business she didn't take into account that some customers would desire to incorporate their own personal style. Consequently, in doing so it would require extra time for labor intensive design details, and Marge's flat fee method didn't allocate for this. Needless to say, Marge had no frame of reference as to her actual production time, and therefore underestimated the time it would take her to complete the project. Let's examine the elements of Marge's problem.

Standard Item: *Her standard retail item consisted of a simple little girl's pinafore that took her no more than two hours to produce. The appeal for this item was in the way that she merchandised it over dresses through the use of vibrant colors and soft pastels. She would show the versatility gained in putting a pinafore over a little girls dress thus creating an entirely different look. She used color as a strong enticement. Occasionally she would add simple embellishments, however, nothing to the extent of what her customer ordered.*

Customer: *Ms. Wallingford, an affluent executive at Transcontinental Bank, had three granddaughters ranging from three to five years old. She had seen Marge's pinafores at a birthday party one of her customers had given. Her customer's daughter, Heather—six years old, was wearing one of Marge's standard pinafores in a pretty emerald green over a soft-pastel gingham dress. Being impressed with Marge's pinafores and eye for color, Ms. Wallingford booked an appointment with Marge.*

Customer's Order: *Three pinafores and three dresses, one for each granddaughter. The bodice would be smocked with contrasting thread to match the pinafore. Instead of a simple hem, she wanted a delicate lace trim. The dresses were simple and required nothing out of the ordinary. It was Marge's basic dress pattern that she used for all her retail orders.*

Labor Charges: *Marge charged her standard flat fee for the dresses, which was sufficient. She charged her standard flat fee for three of the pinafores.*

Problem: *It takes Marge two hours of production time to make each standard pinafore (no embellishments). Each pinafore with smocking and lace required an additional hour and a half, bringing the labor intensive design details to 4 ½ extra hours. Her flat fee method did not allow for the added production time, nor did she consider that fact when giving her client a completion time. Marge did not meet deadline, and had to call several customers to reschedule pick up times. Marge lost one of her very best customers in the process—Mrs. Cunningham. Marge wasn't aware that Mrs. Cunningham needed her daughter's pinafore to wear to a wedding.*

Marge's Loss: *First and foremost, she lost the integrity of her word; a valued customer, not to mention the financial loss suffered for inappropriate pricing. She endured stress from trying to meet an impossible deadline, and had to suffer feelings of helplessness.*

Marge's Labor Calculations

Project	*Production Time*	*Labor Charge*	*3 Pinafores*
Standard Pinafore: Flat Fee	*2.0 hours*	*$35.00*	*$105.00*
Smocking + Lace Trim	*1.5 hours*	*26.25*	*$78.75*
Standard + Smocking + Lace Trim	*3.5 hours*	*$61.25*	*$183.75*

Financial Loss			
Customer's Order	**Actual Production Cost**	**Billed Customer**	**Total Monetary Loss**
3 Pinafores/Smocking/Lace Trim	*$61.25 x 3 = $183.75*	*$35.00 x 3 = $105.00*	*$183.75 - $105.00 = $78.75*

Using the flat fee method, Marge only charged for the standard pinafore. Thus, creating a loss of $78.75 in total profit because her flat fee method did not allow for the labor intensive design details of smocking and lace trim.

Production Loss		
Actual Production Time	**Billed Hours**	**Total Hourly Loss**
3.5 hours x 3 = 10.5 hours	*2.0 hours x 3 = 6.0 hours*	*10.5 – 6.0 = 4.5 hours*

Marge lost 4.5 hours in total production caused by the extra labor intensive design details of smocking and lace trim. This loss could have yielded her 2 1/4 pinafores at the standard pinafore production time of $78.75 profit.

Note: See Marge's revised "Custom Sewing Price List" in Chapter 10

By The Hour Method

Sabrina C.

Sabrina worked part time in a dog grooming salon. She always loved dogs, and over the years had groomed a number of show dogs for affluent customers who placed their pets in competition. Sabrina had sewn for a number of years; never specializing in any one particular field. Her dream was to start a sewing business; however, she had not a clue as to what type of business she wanted.

One afternoon a customer approached her to inquire about finding someone to sew an outfit for his dog. Never having sewn for show dogs, she wasn't quite sure what was involved. Knowing that dogs come in a number of shapes and sizes she felt it would be too risky to charge a flat fee.

Over the next few days she began to develop a measurement chart of the various dogs she groomed in the salon. She made notes of what she felt would be required to sew for show dogs. She had great difficulty finding standard patterns for dogs. After exhausting all possibilities, she decided to draft a prototype in several sizes from muslin. She timed her production and made notes of all the challenges she faced.

Realizing how specialized this field is, and the fact that few sewing professionals embraced this type of work, she knew she had stumbled upon a fortune. "That was it! I will start a business specializing in sewing for show dogs," said Sabrina. She contacted the owner of the salon and negotiated a referral fee for letting her promote her business in the salon. Her first customer was the man who was the genesis of her new business endeavor.

First Project: The customer ordered a custom overcoat with leg extensions. He wanted the fabric to be Scottish plaid with braided trim. He didn't even flinch when Sabrina told him that she charged by the hour.

Pricing Strategy: Based on her research, she new the demand for her expertise, and the limited supply of sewing professionals in this discipline, afforded her the opportunity to use the By The Hour Method. Supply and demand eliminated price resistance because she marketed to consumers who had the discretionary dollars to support her business.

Revenue Streams: From experience with the muslin samples and working with her first customer, she found it was easy to make retail items and sell them in the salon. This was another way of promoting her new business. It brought her customers who wanted customized items for their dogs and she made money on the retail items at the same time.

Sabrina Expands: Within the first year she solicited other dog grooming salons with affluent clientele. She subcontracted out work to other sewing professionals to keep pace with the demand for her services. She produced and marketed her own line of show dog patterns. She started a franchise by licensing and training her subcontractors in their own businesses.

Serendipity or Business Savvy? When asked whether it was serendipity or business-savvy that made her business so successful she replied: It was a bit of both. If my customer had not inquired about my sewing for him, the concept may not have come to me, or at least not that soon. Also, being in a business where my clients frequent didn't hurt. I also did research to determine how to price such a unique product and service. Once I found out how difficult it was to find patterns and people who specialized in the field, I knew that the by the hour method would not cause me any real price resistance. Furthermore, I had the clientele who were willing to meet my prices. The franchise was icing on the cake.

Integrated Pricing Method

Mark P.

Mark's father died when he was very young. Unfortunately, the social security benefits were not sufficient for his mother to provide for him and his two sisters. His mother took on odd sewing jobs to help keep a roof over their heads and eventually opened her own business. She would teach each one of her children how to sew in order to help her with the steady stream of work coming in. Mark objected to helping his mother with her sewing business, saying that sewing is for girls and any boy who sewed was a sissy! Nevertheless, Mark ended up learning to sew in order to help keep food on the table.

All the stress and pressures of trying to raise three children with only one income took its toll on Mark's mother and she suffered a severe stroke, leaving her paralyzed and unable to sew. Mark, being the only boy, took it upon himself to oversee his mothers sewing business. Through the years, despite his resistance, Mark had managed to become extremely good. During his senior year he made a tuxedo for the winter formal.

Not having any real knowledge about business, Mark's mother essentially gave away her professional knowledge and expertise by pricing her goods and services under value. Mark knew that he and his sisters were pretty good at what they did and had no trouble getting business. However, they knew very little about the actual running of a business. Immediately Mark got information and counseling from the Small Business Administration (SBA). He got a business license and renamed the business.

The girls would continue to sew and keep the current stable of customers and new business fluid, while Mark worked on the pertinent business issues associated with running a business. He made himself president and assigned his eldest sister as comptroller. His younger sister was creative and personable, so he trained her to handle all the advertising and customer service issues.

Going through the SBA taught Mark one very valuable skill—how to price for profit. Mark learned a number of pricing methods. One stuck in his mind more than the others—the Integrated Pricing Method. He recalled the number of hours his mother would spend with her customers just going over what was best for their figures types and lifestyle…she was actually consulting with her customers and never got compensated for it in her pricing. Not only was she cheated with respect to consultation, she undercharged for the production on the project—a mistake Mark and his sisters would not make!

First Step: To implement the integrated pricing method, Mark knew that he would have to come up with a figure to use as a multiplier. He used a pricing formula to help him achieve his goals. He needed to determine production time needed for units and items and would find this by utilizing the time and motion study. Each sibling would time the other with the use of a watch or clock with a second hand. He also needed a price list worksheet to track item and unit production, and then use his figure from the pricing formula to multiply total item and unit cost. He and his sisters made a project and task list as a tool to conduct the time and motion study to determine production time needed for items and units. From the price list worksheet they would construct a final price list.

Challenge: Mark and his two sisters had different skill levels, and their production time to complete an item or unit would vary. He needed to determine whether a division of labor was the best option, or take an average of all three of their production times. Finally, he decided that it would be in the best interest of the company to average all three time and motion studies. This way it didn't matter who produced the item or the unit, it would all average out and the company would not suffer. The good news is that Mark and his sisters were equally talented in all fields, and actual production time didn't vary a great deal.

Meeting Both Goals: Consultation represented a large part of their business. Knowing that they also produced a product as well as provided a service, Mark wanted a system to allow him to do both without compromising profit. With the integrated pricing method he was able to accomplish both.

How To Use Pricing Methods Effectively

Flat Fee: The flat fee pricing method is for a business that is standardized with no variations in their product offerings. Your price list includes all the items you produce with no additional design details—no changes! Marge, Sabrina and Mark had three very different pricing methods. Marge used the flat fee method which allows you to charge a flat fee for an item. This method works best when you have made allowances for all the variables in your business. If Marge makes standard items and includes all the variables in her price list this method could work. However, it would mean that she would have to revise her flat fee price list if she decided to take on a project with additional design details that had not been covered. For example, the client who wanted special embellishments on the pinafores. Marge's flat fee price list did not allow for these design changes.

Sewing professionals who have truly defined what they will sew, and never take on projects that aren't on their price list, can make the flat fee method work beautifully for them. But they must understand that it limits them in being able to take on projects with labor intensive design details that have not been allocated in their flat fee pricing structure. If your flat fee price doesn't include smocking and adding lace trim, and you want to take on this kind of a project, it means you must decline or go back and revise your standard price list. If you want to have the flexibility to incorporate your clients personal style on a project, then the flat fee method is not for you. Marge did decide that the flat fee pricing structure was the one for her business. To see how it worked for her, refer to the chapter on *Sewing For Children*.

By The Hour: One of the most effective ways of utilizing this method is when you find a niche where there is a limited supply of sewing professionals in the discipline, and the demand for the goods and services are high. Case in point was Sabrina, who started a business sewing for show dogs and later sold franchise opportunities. Having such a specialized field afforded her the opportunity to use the By The Hour Method. Supply and demand eliminated price resistance because she marketed to consumers who had the discretionary dollars to support her business.

Another example of the effective use of this method is brilliantly executed by Susan Khalje. Take a look at her pricing examples in the chapter on *Sewing For The Bride*. Her work is so exquisite and specialized that she can command the kind of income that by the hour yields. In this particular example, it is not that the principle of supply and demand are in effect, it is Susan's unique talent, knowledge and expertise that influence the ultimate consumer to do business with her. She is an artist. Her clients recognize her value, and therefore don't mind paying her for it.

Integrated Pricing Method: Mark P's business is an excellent example of where the integrated pricing method worked extremely well. Experience and research has shown that one of the reasons to use this method is when you are providing a good as well as a service. The method offers a great degree of flexibility with respect to your ability to take on labor intensive design detailed projects without compromising your value. You are assured that you will never cheat yourself or feel underpaid because the integrated pricing method incorporates several elements of pricing as a form of insurance. Another attractive benefit lies in the fact that the client can get involved in the pricing process. If he or she has a budget and goes over by selecting a number of design details, they can elect to eliminate certain details, thus bringing them back into their budget. It's a win-win situation for both you and the client. You are not getting cheated, and the client still gets to have you make the project.

Pricing Formula

Why do we need a pricing formula? We need to have a multiplying factor to figure labor cost. Once we can establish how much production time we need to complete an item or project we will multiply it by the base labor rate also known as the base hourly rate. This figure is established through the pricing formula. When used in conjunction with the integrated pricing method, the rate is hidden in the total price of the project. It will make sense once we see how to develop a price list using the time and motion study. The following are components of the pricing formula.

> ## There are three components needed:
> 1. Total cost of overhead expenses
> 2. Total hours committed to your business
> 3. Your desired salary

The total cost of overhead expenses involves such things as rent/lease, phone, utilities, etc. It does not take into consideration the fabric and notions purchased for your clients. Those items are called direct expenses and shall be billed back to the client on the invoice.

Total hours committed to your business is just that, you select a given number of hours that you will commit to your business every month. This insures the health, profitability and growth of the business—the operative word is commit!

Your desired salary: When working with my clients (as a business consultant), I have found that most people have preconceived ideas about how much they wish to have in profits at the end of the month. This figure becomes your monthly salary, just as if you were working for someone else and getting paid. If you exceed your goals, everything else is icing on the cake. To demonstrate the pricing formula we will use the following charts:

The "3" Components To The Pricing Formula
1. Overhead expense
2. Hours committed
3. Desired salary

Formula	Component Values	Example
Overhead expenses + desired salary Divided by hours committed = base hourly rate	1.Overhead expense - $975 2.Hours committed – 160 per mo. 3.Desired salary- $4,000	$975 + $4,000 160 hrs

---

How To Calculate The Base Hourly Rate	
1) $4,000 + 975 $4,975	2) $4,975 Divided by 160 hrs. = $31.09 3) Round up to $32 dollars base hourly rate

---

Calculating Production Time

It is amazing the number of sewing professionals who do not know their actual production time. In order to formulate a price list you must have knowledge of how long it takes you to complete a project. You will need to have time frames for small labor intensive details, such as zippers, hooks and eyes, buttons and so on. The method most widely used in business to determine production time is known as a Time and Motion Study. Corporations pay large sums of money to have these studies conducted. It is not difficult to accomplish; however, it does require some of your precious time.

Time and Motion Study

You will need the following to perform the study and make your price list:
1. Project and Task List
2. Time and Motion Chart
3. Price List Worksheet
4. Watch or Clock with second hand
5. Preferably someone to time you
6. Base hourly rate

Form Elements

To conduct a time and motion study you will need three forms: *Project and Task List*; *Time and Motion Chart*; and the *Price List Worksheet*. In *The "Business" Of Sewing* book, I demonstrated the relationship and functionality of these forms. For those of you who do not have that text, I have listed the form elements and will give examples of each form.

Note: if you do not wish to reinvent the wheel, these forms can be found in the *Complete Set Of Forms* or *Forms on Computer Disk*, see the order form at the end of this book. For a complete explanation of all 23 forms, see the chapter on business tools.

Form Elements		
Project and Task List	*Time and Motion Chart*	*Price List Worksheet*
Initial Preparation Construction: 　a. item 　b. unit Finishing	Time 　a. start 　b. stop Grand Total	Project/Task Type Total Time Total Time x Base Rate 　(base hourly rate)

Purpose of the Forms

Project and Task List: This is used to list all of the functions you will perform with respect to labor on your project. You will list them in three categories: Initial Preparation involves everything needed to start construction. Some professionals put in their initial consultation and measurement time here. Construction, both as an item and as a unit. We want item figures so we can charge for small labor intensive design details when needed. And last, Finishing, these are all the tasks performed to get the project ready for completion. Some people place pick-up time in this section. Those who specialize in home décor might put their installation time here. What you decide to put on this form is personal and relates to the type of business you conduct. The example of the Project and Task List, is just that—an example. Yours will be different.

Time and Motion Chart: This is the tool used to actually access true production time. To keep the study pure, you start the clock and stop it whenever you receive an interruption or take a break. Although you may be performing your study on a unit; you will derive the small labor intensive design details (items) needed for your miscellaneous column on your price list. These are such things as buttons, hook and eyes, snaps, zippers, matching stripes and plaids, and anything you think will be an item pricing element on your final price list. Remember, we need to know production time for construction as both an item and a unit for pricing our labor.

Price List Worksheet: This is the final form needed to develop your final price list. You will take the figures from the "total time column" of your time and motion chart and put them in the column labeled "total time" on your price list worksheet. Once you have all the labor figures for item as well as units, you will use your base hourly rate to figure what your labor charges should be. Remember that the base hourly rate, or base rate, comes from your pricing formula which was discussed earlier in this chapter. Below are examples of: 1. Project and Task List   2. Time and Motion Chart   3. Price List Worksheet

PROJECT AND TASK LIST

INITIAL PREPARATION	CONSTRUCTION 1 [As An Item]	CONSTRUCTION 2 [As A Unit]	FINISHING
FABRIC PREPARATION	BODICE	SKIRT	HEMS
PATTERN PREPARATION	SLEEVE	PANTS	BUTTONS
LAYOUT	COLLAR	DRESS	BUTTONHOLES
CUTTING	FACINGS	JACKET	HOOK/EYES
MARKING	LINING	BLOUSE	TOPSTITCHING
	SKIRT SEAMS/DARTS		PRESSING
	PANT SEAMS/DARTS		
	WAIST BANDS	COMPLETE THE LIST BY ADDING TASK	
	ZIPPER INSERTION	RELATIVE TO YOUR BUSINESS.	

Time and Motion Chart

Time		Time and Motion Study	Total Time
Start	Stop	Project/Task: Straight Skirt	Hours/Minutes
8:15	10:15	Fabric & pattern preparation, layout, cutting, marking	2 Hours
10:30	11:30	Seams/ darts/ zipper/press	1
12:30	2:30	Sewed lining, fused interfacing to waistband, applied label, attached band to skirt and lining unit, press	2
3:00	4:00	Hem both units, applied button and buttonholes, final pressing	1
Grand Total			6 Hours

Price List Worksheet

PROJECT/TASK	TYPE	TOTAL TIME	TOTAL TIME X
SKIRT (LINED)	STRAIGHT	6	$ 114.00
SKIRT	STRAIGHT	3	57.00
PANTS (LINED)	PLEATED	5	95.00
DRESS	A-LINED	6	114.00
JACKET (LINED)	TAILORED	7	133.00
JACKET	TAILORED	6	114.00
BLOUSE	SHELL	3	57.00

COMPONENTS OF A PRICE LIST

	UNLINED	LINED	
PANTS			
TAILORED W/O PCKTS	50.00	60.00	
DRESSES			
BASE PRICE	60.00	70.00	
JACKETS	UNLINED	LINED	
TAILORED (BASIC)	90.00	100.00	

A

MISCELLANEOUS	UNLINED	LINED
SHOULDER PADS/UNCOVERED	10.00	
SEAMS (ADDITIONAL)	9.00	
FRONT FLY ZIPPER	8.00	8.00
DESIGN LININGS (COATS, JACKETS)	10.00	
DESIGN LININGS (SKIRTS, PANTS)	8.00	
PRE-SHRINKING FABRIC (PER YARD)	1.10	
BUTTONHOLES (EACH)	1.50	
BUTTONS (EACH)	1.20	
VENT, FLAP (EACH)	7.00	7.00
PATCH POCKETS (EACH)	7.00	7.00
WELT POCKETS (EACH)	10.00	10.00

D

ALTERATIONS	UNLINED	LINED
HEMS	12.00	22.00
SLEEVES-HEM	10.00	20.00
SLEEVES REWORK	15.00	25.00
SLEEVES TAPER	10.00	20.00
SHOULDER SEAMS	10.00	20.00
SHOULDER SEAMS W/FACING	15.00	25.00
CROTCH W/O ZIPPER	10.00	20.00
CROTCH W/ZIPPER	20.00	30.00
ZIPPERS (SKIRT/PANTS)	10.00	15.00
ZIPPERS (LEATHER/SUEDE)	13.00	18.00
ZIPPERS (DRESS)	15.00	20.00
SIDE SEAMS W/O BAND (SKIRT/PANTS)	15.00	25.00
SIDE SEAMS W/BAND)(SKIRT/PANTS)	20.00	30.00

E

CONSULTATION	PRICES
PER HOUR	19.00
INITIAL (UP-TO-AN-HOUR)	19.00
(WAIVED IF SERVICES ACCEPTED-AND APPLIED TO FINAL BILL)	

F

SEWING LESSONS		
PRIVATE (PER HOUR)	19.00	
GROUP RATES 2 TO 10 PEOPLE	15.00	PER PERSON
GROUP RATES 11+ PEOPLE	12.00	PER PERSON
(GROUP SESSIONS ARE HELD ON GROUP SITE)		

G

ON SITE FEES	
UP TO ONE (1) MILE	2.00
TWO (2) TO FIVE (5) MILES	4.00
SIX (6) TO TEN (10) MILES	6.00
ELEVEN (11) OR MORE (PER MILE)	1.00

H

ADDED FEATURES: PRICE SUBJECT TO DESIGN

Making Your Personal Price List

From the *Price List Worksheet*, you will organize all the information into specific categories that will be easy to work with (see Components of a Price List). You will need two columns, one for lined and the other for unlined pricing. We must not forget that lining is labor intense and we must be compensated for our time. It is best to keep item pricing in separate categories such as miscellaneous, these are the elements of your pricing structure that will be added on as you are using the integrated pricing method. If you are using any other method, it serves as an excellent tool for keeping accurate records of what you should be charging to make a profit and recover overhead expenses. If you are not covering both of these goals then you need to reevaluate your pricing structure.

Note: You should develop a mileage or on-site fee for going to the customer's home or place of business. If you teach sewing, develop prices for classes for both individual and group sessions. From time to time you will do alterations, so make a section just for alterations and include it on your price list. In many instances I have done wardrobe consultations for my clients; because we do consultation we should have a section for consultations. Some professionals prefer to put consultations associated with projects inside of their "initial preparations" on their *Project and Task List*. This can be risky if you do not control the consultation session with the client. If you know that it takes you approximately 30 minutes, you must ensure that you do not run over, especially if this has been built into your price list. I personally do not build in consultation, as I have found that I only cheat myself. When consultation is linked to the actual production on a project, I bill that as a separate unit and collect it up front in the clerical phase of the interview. It will appear on the clients total invoice as a credit. I use the *Consultation/Work Agreement* a.k.a. contract to accomplish my goal. * These forms can be found in the *Complete Set Of Forms* or *Forms on Computer Disk*, see the order form at the end of this book.

DESCRIPTION FOR THE COMPONENTS OF A PRICE LIST

 From the Price List Worksheet, you will organize all the information into specific categories that will be easy to work with.

 You will need two columns. The first column of your price sheet will be for unlined pricing.

 The second column is for lined pricing. We must not forget that lining is labor intense and we must be compensated for our time.

 Keep item pricing in a separate category such as miscellaneous. These are the elements of your pricing structure that will be added on as you are using the integrated pricing method.

 Often clients will want changes on a project after it's finished or they will gain or lose weight. Then it's an alteration; so make a section just for alterations and include it on your price list.

 In many instances you will only consult with your clients; be sure to remember to acknowledge how important that fee is and have a section for consultations.

 If you teach sewing, develop prices for classes for both individual and group sessions.

Develop a mileage or on-site fee for going to the customer's home or place of business. If you shop for them out of your normal radius charge them mileage and consultation.

Sewing Meets Retail Sales and Services

Can You Sew for Profit & Sell Other Products?

Can you sew for profit and combine other business endeavors? A number of sewing professionals engage in other retail sales and services: cosmetics, skin care, jewelry, candles, real estate, household products and a number of other profitable ventures.

Bonnie L. Motts was ingenious in finding her dual niche; combining sewing for profit with retail sales and services. Bonnie is a professional image consultant, fashion coordinator, couture designer-dressmaker, skin care specialist, and make-up artist. She provides these services to men, women, and teens, offering the *Total Image Solution—From Head to Toe*. It's not just a quick-fix, but a training on how *to "Become The Best You Can Be."* In addition to her custom sewing and design services, Bonnie offers training, workbooks, worksheets, and BeautiControl skin care and cosmetic products. Bonnie explains how she achieved her goals.

During the 70's my husband, newborn daughter and I were stationed in Colorado for a couple of years. What a great experience! We lived in an apartment complex. During the day I would explore the area with my daughter. While sightseeing one day, I came across another military lady who had started her own sewing business. I decided to take some classes from her on lingerie, knit, swimwear, and how to copy patterns. This was perhaps one of the spark plugs that got me so interested in starting a sewing business.

She had an Elna sewing machine that did everything. I raved to my husband about what I could accomplish with this machine. I only had a straight-stitch basic off-brand machine; and the Elna was just what I needed. The new machine cost $350 dollars, and my husband's entire army salary for the month was only $425, which had to cover a furnished one bedroom apartment, feed a family of three and allow us to do some extra things. My husband made the comment: "Are you really going to use this machine?" Well, that was a dare; I thought to myself, "I'll start a small business right from our apartment!"

I proceeded to develop a price list for doing minor alterations and repairs, while keeping my eyes open to what other people were charging. At the time, my prices ranged from $1.00 to $25.00 for repairs. I was comparing what retail garments cost. After all I wasn't an expert, at least I didn't think so. I was just learning. WRONG! I thought I was justified for thinking that way.

I wanted to teach so I presented some garments I had made to the sewing machine dealer where I purchased my machine. He hired me on the spot to teach his clients how to use their new Elna sewing machines. I just loved teaching, it was so natural for me. Shortly thereafter, a school teacher paid me from her salary to teach unwed mothers the basics of sewing. I also continued to take sewing classes. Keeping up-to-date and gaining knowledge is so valuable for anyone in business. My expertise started to grow, but there were still so many things to learn.

In order to take in alterations, repairs, and custom sewing projects, I put cards on bulletin boards with my contact information. I did not advertise my price list. Military wives and soldiers who needed repairs or new patches became my clients.

I soon developed a nice client base with a couple of real classy customers who brought me nothing but Vogue patterns (my first real introduction to Vogue). They were the hardest patterns around with their unusual details. It took me twice as long, but did I ever learn. One of my clients brought me an interlined and lined dress and jacket pattern that had 32 bound buttonholes. Yes, I said 32! I explained to her that I needed to examine the pattern in order to give her a price. I was horrified; I had never done a bound buttonhole before—let alone 32. I couldn't price it. I thought that $1.00 per buttonhole would be fair. I didn't even consider the other detail work, since most of the garments that I made for this customer were in the

$25 to $30 range. I was afraid to quote her much higher because she might not pay it, so I quoted $35.00 for everything.

While working on the project, I started to measure the time that it took me to accomplish various parts of a garment and kept records for future use. I worked very hard on that entire outfit, and probably made a better bound buttonhole than I could even now since I haven't had as much practice lately. I was really glad when that project was over because my profit was *&^/^^#/. My client was pleased, needless to say, and of course she told someone else about what I had made. I gained other clients. Still feeling afraid that I might loose my client base, I did learn to go up in my pricing slightly, making an average of $2.00 an hour—if I was lucky. My profit margin wasn't there, and I soon found myself sewing all the time. When our two years were up in Colorado, I had to disband my business, and go back to Ohio. I got a job at a small sewing center, and taught for another Elna dealer. I also held classes from my home, and did sewing for a few word-of-mouth clients. My pricing was now averaging $5 to $8 per hour, which wasn't too bad for the mid 70's. While I taught, I made detailed notes and illustrations to use for my classes, sample garments in every stage, and developed my own style. I am a very detailed person.

I did it all, alterations, custom work and started doing some interior design while developing my own price list. As an avid reader of sewing books, I tried to learn all I could about designing and found that I had a gift for constructing garments from scratch by designing my own patterns from photos. My confidence level was growing by leaps and bounds. In 1972, we finally purchased our first home. Soon I got into interior design by making my custom window treatments. Shortly thereafter, I was being called upon to help others to design window treatments, remodel and wallpaper their homes. I became an expert, and did many jobs during those early years. Some of the my clients have contacted me for consultation with them on what styles I would recommend, or to help them with layout and design of their new kitchen (of course I charge a consulting fee). On the whole, I do not take on custom interior design jobs, however, I have for some of my special clients.

As the 80's approached and my family grew, I started to feel overwhelmed with more responsibility, and not seeing my dreams formulate. I made a decision to get more focused on quality garments and not just quick sewing. To update my sewing knowledge, I decided to take a seminar at Ann Hyde Haute Couture School of Fashion Design. Shortly thereafter, I studied at the Fashion Institute of Technology and Design, in New York City. New York was an exciting city and my interest really piqued for fashion and image programs. I started with my own personal image and soon started to put more emphasis toward the overall picture that would develop into my future business. I started working more with color, and made a concerted effort to work on becoming the best I could be. I improved my personal style, and expanded my knowledge of sewing and image consulting.

My clients started requesting me to take a more active role in their personal shopping, doing their makeup, or giving them instruction on what to do for special occasions. It didn't take me long to figure out that I was missing out on some things: more items to sell. The search began for a company that could sell me product wholesale. I soon found out that *I really wasn't a store,* and couldn't afford to take on such large inventories. However, there was a company that was involved in color and body analysis, sold skin care products, and color-coded cosmetics. They dealt with the *Total Image Package.* This seemed to be more affordable. They offered a training package without the demands of product ordering.

In 1990, I signed up to be a consultant with BeautiControl Cosmetics. I had no idea I would enjoy the training I received and would soon develop a new client base for cosmetics and skin care. I never wanted to sell anything, but I soon realized that we are selling ourselves each and every day even though we are not in sales. Later, I went to Dallas for their leadership training program which helped me focus on learning retail sales, product knowledge, fashion, image, and professionalism in the workplace.

My first year in retail, along with my sewing, almost tripled my income. My clients wanted one-on-one sessions. I charged $50 toward product and scheduled three one-hour sessions with them for a total of $200 per session, and made an additional $80 to $100 in actual retail sales. Every woman needed what I had to offer. I found a little niche in the sewing market that developed into a wonderful business where I didn't have to stay exclusively in my sewing studio. Retail can bring clients back, if you are selling something they need.

My business increased significantly when I started to teach and hold personal and group consultation sessions for men, women, teens, organizations, and corporations. While giving my seminars and workshops, I developed workbooks and materials that I could personally copyright for my classes. My pricing method for my sewing is by far more detailed. I now have sewing clients who desire image consultation and vice versa. I can pick and choose my jobs.

The 90's brought on a new image for my business. My business cards changed from Bon's Place to *Bon's Place "Your Total Image Studio"*. I took on the motto "Become The Best You Can Be" and finally found what I wanted to do. Experiences in your life can help you to grow more than you can imagine.

I still do alterations, specialty items, bridal, and custom sewing, but I only take on what I can handle because of my consultations and extensive teaching schedule. I charge more for my workmanship, and if a client doesn't want to pay $20 dollars for a hem done on a silk garment, I don't worry about it. I always hand pick the stitches with care, and if they want a $6 hem done they can go to the dry cleaners! I require more than minimum wage.

In your business, if you do quality work why shouldn't you be paid for it? I found that you are not going to make everyone happy. You will make mistakes—so forgive yourself, and move on. My client base is not what it was back in the 70's, but my clients do pay more. Some have left only to return when they found out that some people just sew and some, like me, do intricate workmanship.

Most people that appreciate quality, buy quality garments and want someone they can trust to alter their expensive garments. Just make sure that you can handle the project. You need to be the expert at what you do and make sure your workmanship reflects it. If the task is beyond your level of sewing expertise, than pass it up in order to prevent chatter regarding your poor skills. I truly love what I am doing and I am always striving to do more, so my growth is just beginning and I have so much more to accomplish in the next 20 years.

Quick Tips For Business Growth And Development

- Develop written goals.
- Never downplay your business!
- Devise a workable business plan.
- Plan a great promotion for yourself.
- Never forget about returning phone calls.
- Keep trying to grow by trying new things.
- Do what you love and the money will follow.
- Don't forget that for every action there is an end result.
- Promote yourself through your appearance in and out of your studio.
- Don't give yourself unreasonably short time frames to accomplish what you desire.

Following these tips will help you to realize your goals, stay more focused and develop stability.

Initially I used my home number, business cards, and word of mouth as my advertisement. Later, I purchased a new computer system with a laser printer so that I could start making my own brochures and worksheets, I also purchased a fax machine, copier, cellular phone, pager, and business phone. With a business number, I could get into the yellow page listings and have a nice ad (at least the first time around) for a much lower rate. I had one for Canton, Akron, and then Massillon. What a cost! With Yellow Pages ads and listings comes more debt every month you operate your business. Each year I went to a smaller ad in order to cut my cost. I do get results from these ads though. Now I am on the Internet. You can find me at mottsbon_@beauti.com or bonniemotts@beaut.com.

New changes in your business will take more time. Figure on working 15 to 18 hour days if you are lucky. Computers are great, but you need to learn how to use them. They're good for entering your client base, mass mailings or doing your inventory. It took me forever to get the inventory in plus the usage of the program. Working on the Internet takes time. Time! Time! Time! It all takes Time! You could hire someone to do this for you, but what if you can't afford to pay someone? Can you afford not to do your job? Well, you will have to stay up nights doing all of the clerical work yourself. Think of bartering your service for someone else's time. This has helped people in the past. Don't forget to ask! You have to be a little brave, but remember: they can only say NO. It is only "no" and not the end of the world. Now that you are really serious about your business, consider raising your prices, taking on more jobs, or hiring people to work for you. If you hire others remember you are opening up a new can of worms.

Bonnie's Pieces and Parts Pricing—Women

Points to remember:

- What will you charge for consultation time?
- Any extra consultations and fittings needed, and if you are charging by the hour. I can give my clients a fairly close range of prices using the hourly method.
- Consider your pricing for odd jobs or specialty items. Give yourself either $8 to $10 per hour or $10 to $15 as the average figure for garment construction plus other sessions. In reality you could make $15 to $30 per hour.
- Figure on the high side for hours of time for garment construction. Consider fabric, details, pattern work, consultations, fabric shopping, extra notions and anything else that is pertinent. Take your pieces and parts pricing sheet and figure up a general cost analysis on some of the details in the construction of the garment.
- Quote prices that are possibly 2 to 3 hours higher at the hourly rate in order to justify changes or difficulty—especially if you haven't selected the fabric.

Pricing Example:

A party dress might range anywhere from $250 to $300 dollars plus tax and fabric. You will have at least a 3-hour buffer built in either by adding 3 extra hours on to what you are making using the range of $8 to $15 per hour. Most clients don't mind the price range if I say it won't be any higher, and possibly lower depending on the difficulty and fittings (2 fittings are included). I add one more hour in my own calculations for a buffer. I will stay true to my pricing and my clients understand that if they make changes, then extra pricing for time will be added. When the garment actually costs them $265.56, they are happy. I have made my same profit of anywhere from $15 to $30 dollars per hour.

You need to build in some time in order to allow for profit. Sometimes your profit will only be in the range of $8 to $10 dollars, especially if you forget to add a buffer. Don't forget the specialty items that you are adding, such as hand sewing of pearls, details, etc. If you are slow at some of the detail work, then use the lower rate because you will make it up in other construction details. If my projects take a few more hours, it's figured into my basic pieces and parts worksheet plus an additional 2- to 3-hour buffer. I also charge $25 for the initial consultation with $10 going toward the project if I am hired. If you have a client who wants a final price, use the higher figure plus tax. I usually go higher. My customers know I will be fair.

Note: Bonnie's 4 page price list starts on the next page. She has the following:

- ☑ General Cost of Garments—Custom Made
- ☑ Basic Custom Garment Pricing
- ☑ General Sewing Details Pricing
- ☑ Pattern Work—Basic Pricing

My Ad Campaign—Bon's Place

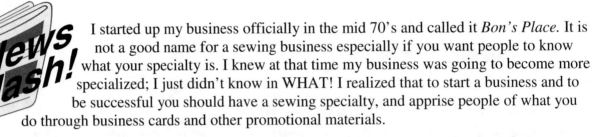 I started up my business officially in the mid 70's and called it *Bon's Place.* It is not a good name for a sewing business especially if you want people to know what your specialty is. I knew at that time my business was going to become more specialized; I just didn't know in WHAT! I realized that to start a business and to be successful you should have a sewing specialty, and apprise people of what you do through business cards and other promotional materials.

My advertising campaign started with a nice ad and a great photo to let people know about my business. Then another great photo was taken and I used it for my business cards and other advertisements. My public saw me with severe slicked back hair and large earrings.

I did seminars, which were paid for by organizations, and I got publicity. I did some free programs and got publicity as well. I worked in conjunction with a photographer to help him with wedding "before and after" photos and got publicity that way too. I kept my face out there for years. I produced and publicized a seminar program entitled "Women of the 90's," in which I spoke about ways to *"Become The Best You Could Be"* and *"How to Make a Lasting Impression"*.

I had to become my own advertising campaign manager to let the public know about my business. I accomplished my goal through direct mailings, professional brochures, and newspaper editorials. It was a really difficult time, but I did learn from that experience what to do and not to do. The rewards from this venture did build my visibility and clientele for many years to follow. People have continued to call because they kept a photo or article about what I did and wanted what I had to offer. The advertising was expensive and I do not advise anyone to do it if you are expecting people to come knocking at their door. You will need to continually stay visible. However, your credibility, workmanship and professionalism will help you build a strong clientele.

Sample Price List 1

Bonnie Motts has perfected her pricing method to a science and the following for list reflects the time and effort she has put into insuring that her pricing method yields her the desired results—a profit!

Bon's Place "Your Total Image Studio"

General Cost of Garments—Custom Made

	Average (Twills, Cottons, Challis)	**Formal, Tailored** (Silky, Sateen, Suiting)
DRESS	$80-125 & up	$120-350 & up
EVENING DRESS		$125-350 & up
WEDDING DRESS		$225-1000 & up
BLOUSE	$50-125 & up	$65-$225 & up
SKIRT	$45-125 & up (straight & gathered)	$65-$200 & up
SLACKS	$55-125 & up	$75 -$200 & up
VEST	$50-100 & up	$65-175 & up
COAT	$180-250 & up	$250-475 & up
JACKET	$90-175 & up	$175-475 & up

*Additional charges for:
pockets, pleats, topstitiching, vents, bias cut, plaids, napped fabrics, extra wide circular hems, collar stays, covered buttons, buttonholes, ruffles, gathers, tucks, longer than street-length designs, hand sewn zippers, shoulder pads, shields, bra strap stays, elastic, flat-felled seams, pockets, yokes, monogramming, beading, boning, lined, sleeve vents, certain fabrics, or any other detail out of the ordinary.

*Additional charges for Pattern Work averages--$50-$125
*Travel to get Material is $25 plus $25 for the first hour and $15 for each additional.
    (when shared with other client purchases--averages $10 / hour)
*Extra changes are either done by the hour or by cost sheeting for special tasks.
    (hourly average is $15 / hour)

Sample Price List 2

Bon's Place "Your Total Image Studio"

General Sewing Details Pricing

Hand Sewing.................(trim to be sewn)............. $5.00 / 48" section
Taking out sewing.............(regular straight stitch)..... $2.00 / 48" section (1 row)
                        (chain stitch)................ $1.00 / 48" section (1 row)

Sew By Machine................(Straight sewing up to 48").. $2.00 & up
                        (Topstitching up to 48")...... $2.50 & up

Buttonholes.....................(Bound)........................ $6.00
                        (Keyhole-hand-done)........ $5.00
                        (Keyhole-machine)........... $4.00
                        (Machine)..................... $1-2.00

Pockets.........................(Flaps)........................ $5.00 each
                        (Welt).......................... $10-15 each
                        (Side).......................... $8.00 for 2
                        (Continental).................. $10.00 for 2
                        (Watch)....................... $5.00 each
                        (Patch)........................ $5.00 each

Belt Loops... $1.00 each

Belts...........................(Corded)..................... $5.00
                        (Soft).......................... $6.00 & up
                        (Stiff)......................... $10-15 plus buckle

Sleeves..........................(Basic set in, off shoulder).. $10-15
                        (Cuffs added, welt, ruffle).. $15-25
                        (Extra details)................ $10-15 additional

Collars..........................(Soft ruffled)................ $10-15
                        (Structured, tailored)......... $15-25

*An initial consultation charge for customers is $25 for a 2 hour consultation to discuss the plans for new custom design or for re-make of garment.
*$10 from the initial consultation fee will go toward the project if a contract is signed.

Sample Price List 3

Bon's Place "Your Total Image Studio"

Basic Custom Garment Pricing

Basic Dress sleeveless.......	(2 piece).......................	$55
	(3 piece).......................	$65
	(4 piece).......................	$70
	(5-7 piece)....................	$85

Basic Blouse sleeveless......	(2 pieces).....................	$20
	(3 pieces).....................	$25
	(4 pieces).....................	$30
	(5-6 pieces)..................	$40

| Basic Skirt straight........... | (knit or woven-2 piece)...... | $35-50 & up |
| | (knit or woven-3 piece)...... | $45-65 & up |

| Basic Slacks................... | (knit-4 pieces)............... | $45-55 & up |
| | (woven-4-6 pieces)........... | $55-75 & up |

*Lining, interlining & underlining construction.............. double Basic

*Fitting discount for 2 fittings only............................ add $10.00
*Additional fittings.. $15.00 / hour

*Pattern Work.................. (1 hour included in basic)....
         (extra pattern work)........... add on from pricing sheet

*Shopping for Fabric..............(Travel Time).............. $25.00
   (minimum of 2hrs.--1st hr.-$25--2nd-$15). $40.00

*Special Fabric adds more to labor time....................... $20-50 more
   (silky, special needs or difficult fabric to sew)

*Details are extra beyond the basic............................ add on individually
*Changes made throughout project............................ add on
*Notions are extra.. add on

Sample Price List 4

Bon's Place "Your Total Image Studio"

Pattern Work—Basic Pricing

Customers Pattern Used (2-3 fittings, paper & labor)		**Draft From Scratch** (2-3 fittings, paper & labor)
BASIC SLACK....	$35 & up	$50 & up
BASIC SKIRT.....	$20 & up	$35 & up
BASIC TOP........	$35 & up	$50 & up
BASIC JACKET..	$50 & up $40 (Partial)	$100 & up
BASIC COAT.....	$50 & up $40 (Partial)	$100 & up
BASIC DRESS...	$50 & up $45 (Partial)	$75 & up
BRIDAL DRESS.	$50 & up	$100 & up

*Change in commercial pattern add cost to patternwork Labor.
*Additional cost is added to the above pattern work for muslin fabric

Alterations—Making It Work For You

What can we say about alterations, either you love it or you hate it. I remember thinking to myself that I didn't do alterations. Boy was I wrong. While sewing for the bride, I had lots of problems with their weight fluctuating. It wasn't until I had lost 6 hours of production time and more than $700 dollars one quarter that I realized that I was indeed doing alterations, and wasn't getting paid for it. When I had to re-work a bridal gown because my client had gained an enormous amount of weight. I got my act together and developed a price list for doing alterations. The following scenario is from a client whom I had the pleasure of working with as a business consultant. Here is Gail's alteration adventure.

Gail B.

Early one spring afternoon, while working in my office inputting new fabric purchases into the computer, I received a call from a lady who was referred to me by one of my current clients. She wanted me to do alterations for her. She stated that she was very small and none of her clothes fit. My immediate thought was to say, "I am sorry, I don't do alterations." Since she had been referred, I decided to screen her to determine whether I wanted to work for her, and to educate her on my business policies, practices and procedures. Knowing that clients tend to feel you should be cheap, especially if you do alterations, I had to clear up that myth up right away. I didn't want her laboring under false apprehension. I had read Barbara's book, **The "Business" of Sewing** *and hired her for consultation, so I knew how to interact with my new clients. I explained to her that I do charge a consultation fee for the clerical and creative phases of the face-to-face interview. I had learned from Barbara that as sewing professionals we work in two phases: Phase one—the clerical phase—is where we introduce two of our forms, the Business Policy and Consultation/Work Agreement—our contract. In addition, we go over the policies, practices and proce-dures of our business, collect fees for services, etc., which generally takes place in your office. The second phase is the creative phase, which takes place in your sewing studio. That's where you and the client work on pattern and design, fabrication, take measurements, do fittings and so on, and I make sure my time is compensated charging clients for consultation—up front!*

My original thought was to convince the client that she should consider having her clothing cus-tom made to avoid the aggravation of buying a garment only to have it altered. I assumed she had two or three pieces, at the most, that needed alterations. That would be no problem, and thereafter we could be-gin working on a wardrobe plan. When she said she was small, I had no idea how small this lady really was. Much to my surprise, she brought me 36 items to be altered. I practically remade each garment. Not one of them was easy! She reassured me that money was no object. Her father was a successful contrac-tor, and she was his accountant. What did I learn from this experience? How to make a price list for al-terations that worked for me. It wasn't until a month into the project that she booked an appointment for wardrobe planning—much to my relief. From that experience, I learned to love doing alterations.

How To Calculate Labor For Alterations

Gail now has a steady stream of clients who bring her alterations. Pricing for alterations isn't diffi-cult; the first step is to keep accurate records of everything needed to complete the alterations project. Make what we call in the industry, a project and task list (see example in this chapter). Generally the list contains three categories: initial preparation; construction (as an item and as a unit) and final finishing de-tails. For alterations, you need to establish the time it takes you to disassemble the garment, which is part of the initial preparation phase. Once you determined your actual production time you can use the base hourly rate to calculate the labor charge (see pricing formula in this text). Any notions used, such as thread, interfacing, etc., will be charged back to the client as direct expenses.

The following is an example of what would be on a project and task list for alterations similar to those being performed by Gail B. Your project and task list would reflect the actual labor performed on your specific projects.

Sample Project and Task List For Alterations		
Project: Rework Sleeves		
Initial Preparations	*Construction*	*Finishing Details*
disassemble garment	stitch sleeve side seams	hem sleeve
cut fabric	pin base sleeve to bodice	apply buttons
mark fabric	stitch sleeve to bodice	press
apply adjustments	apply shoulder pads	place in plastic bag
Do not forget to list all tasks when making your Project and Task List		

Let's say that you are altering a sleeve. You would conduct a time and motion study from your Project and Task List in order to get your production time (see time and motion study in this text). From the pricing formula, you have gotten your base hourly rate which will be used as a multiplying factor to establish labor charges.

In this example we shall assume that Gail conducted a time and motion study based on the time it took her to rework the sleeves on an alterations project. We will assign 4-hours of production time, with a base hourly rate of $12.00, which was obtained from the pricing formula.

Formula For Calculating Labor:

a. **Production Time x Base Labor Rate = Labor Charge**
b. **Production time = 4 hrs.; base labor rate = $12.00**
c. **4 hrs. x $12.00 = $48.00 labor charge.**

Alterations Price List

The following list are courtesy of Bon's Place *"Your Total Image Studio"*, established by Bonnie L. Motts. Examine the structure of these five list; notice the detailed categories used and how Bonnie has taken the time to brake down her pricing for alterations. Make your list based upon the alteration services you will provide and conduct a time and motion study to determine your pricing. Do not become impatient remember that your initial investment of time will yield remarkable result when it comes to pricing for profit.

Alterations Price List 1

Bon's Place "Your Total Image Studio"

Alterations   Skirts   Price List

HEM... $10.00 & up to $20.00
(straight or slightly fuller up to 40" wide......every 18"---$2.00)

    Straight.. $10.00 & up
    Flared.. $12.00 & up
    Very Flared.. $18.00 & up
                                  (2yds & up fullness)
                                    $22-$24-$26
                                    (6yds & up + hem detail)

    Long skirt cut short................................ $15.00 & up to $25.00
                  (depends on fullness, fabric, detail, lined, etc.)
    Wrap skirt can double price or 1 & 1/2 x reg. skirt ($20.00 & up if lined)
    Rolled hem by hand................................. $18.00 & up
               (40"--Price can double w/ more fullness)
        lined................... $5.00 extra
        w/ kick pleat.......... $2.00 extra
        topstitched............ $3.00 extra
        lengthen and face.... $9.00 & up to $20.00

OTHER Alterations...
    Shorten from waist.................................. $18.00 & up
          move zipper down.................. $5.00 extra
    Drop waistband...................................... $14.00
                      down.......... $19.00

    Waist in... $7.00
          and lined............................. $8.00
          remove waistband.................. $12.00 & up to $18.00
    Sides in... $8.00
        (1 or 2 seams)
        and lined............................. $10.00
        in thru hem or narrow skirt....$12.00 & up to $18.00
        (lined is $4.00 extra)

    Replace zipper.. $8.00 plus zipper
    Replace elastic in waist............................ $6.00 and up
    Replace lining.. $15.00 & up plus lining

Alterations Price List 2

Bon's Place "Your Total Image Studio"

Alterations   (Women's) Pants   Price List

HEM... $10.00 & up
             (shorten or lengthen)

lengthen and face... $4.00 extra
             (plus cost of the bias tape)

lined... $4.00 extra
cuffs... $6.00 extra

Levi jeans (topstitched)............................... $8.00 & up to $15.00
Leather pants (shortened)............................ $12.00 & up

OTHER Alterations...

Taper legs.. $10.00
          and lined............................ $15.00

Sides in.. $8.00 & up
          and lined............................ $9.50 & up

Waist in.. $7.00 & up
          and lined............................ $8.00 & up
          remove waistband................. $10.00 & up to $15.00
          Levi's.............................. $8.00 & up to $15.00
Drop waistband...................................... $12.00
         and move zipper down.............. $17.00

Replace zipper... $9.00 & up plus zipper
         Plastic Jacket zipper.................. $3.00 extra
         Invisible zipper...................... $4.00 extra

Take in stride.. $7.50
Adjust crotch.. $5.00 & up
Re-enforce zipper....................................... $1.00
Redo pockets along with alterations......... $5.00 plus material / pocket
Put in lining... $17.50 plus lining material

Alterations Price List 3

Bon's Place "Your Total Image Studio"

Alterations   Blouses   Price List

HEM.. $6.00 & up
                     (machine straight stitch only)

Shorten sleeves.. $8.00 & up to $18.00
move placket... $4.00 extra
cuffs & tucks... $15-18-20.00

Narrow shoulders..................................... $12-15-20.00
Narrow shoulders w/pads & re-set sleeves.... $20.00 & up plus pads
Narrow shoulder w/tuck............................. $8.00
Add shoulder pads.................................... $5.00 plus pads

Gussets.. $8.00
Sides in... $6.00
Narrow collar.. $6.00
Put in darts.. $4.00
Replace buttons....................................... $ .50 / + button
Make covered buttons............................... $1.00 / button
Make buttonholes (machine made-regular).. $1.00
          (remove old button stitching) $1.00
Replace sleeve elastic................................ $3.00

Dresses

Hem..same as skirt
          (if delicate material, the cost could double)

Sides in through waist.................................... $10.00 & up
Replace zipper... $9.00 & up to $15.00
          (plus the cost of zipper)
Other Alterations.. same as blouse

Alterations Price List 4

Bon's Place "Your Total Image Studio"

Alterations   Blazers   Price List

Shorten Sleeves..	$10 & up
plain..	$10.00
plain w/ lining..	$14.00
plain w/ bias tape edge..............................	$12.00
with vent & buttons (2-4)...........................	$18 & up
with vent and buttons (lined).....................	$20 & up
with vent and buttons (6-8)........................	$19 & up
with vent and buttons (lined).....................	$22 & up
new interfacing added...............................	$1.00 extra
Lengthen Sleeves and face..................................	$12-18 & up
Narrow Sleeves..	$8.00
lined..	$12.00
Sides in...	$6.00
lined..	$8.00
Sides in through armhole....................................	$10.00
lined..	$12.00
Take darts in..	$2.00 / pair
lined..	$4.50 / pair
Take in center back seam...................................	$4.00
lined..	$6.00
thru hemline..	$5.00 extra
Narrow shoulders...	$12.50 & up
lined..	$15-20 & up
with shoulder pads....................................	$4.00 extra
Put in shoulder pads..	$8.00 plus pads
Make an inside pocket..	$8-12 & up
Narrow lapels.....(total collar & lapel)..............	$25-40
lower section of lapels.............................	$10-15
replace topstitching.................................	$6.00
Leather elbow patches..	$12.00 plus patches
Replace buttons...	$ .50 plus buttons
Arm shields...	$6.00
Machine buttonhole..	$2.00 each
Keyhole buttonhole (hand done)..........................	$5.00 each
Bound buttonhole...	$6.00 each
Reline...	$25 plus fabric
Shorten Jacket...	$12-18
lined..	$18-24
vent...	$4.00 extra

Alterations Price List 5

Bon's Place "Your Total Image Studio"

Alterations   Coats   Price List

Alterations	Price List
Hem..	$15-30 (width of 40")
straight...	$15-22
lined...	$18-25
flared..	$18-27
lined...	$20-30
vents...	$5.00 extra
pleats..	$5.00 each
additional width.............................	$6.00 / 20"
Lengthen and face...............................	$20-40
Raincoat Hem.....................................	$17.50-30.00
(pleats, flair, vents extra charge)	
Leather Hem....................................	$25-35
Fur Hem...	$35-40
Shorten Sleeves................................	$10-18
lined...................................	$15-22
Leather jacket sleeves shortened........................	$15-22
lined...................................	$18-24
Raincoat Sleeves shortened................................	$15-20
lined...................................	$18-22
move placket..	$20-24
with buttons..	$4.00 extra
Narrow Sleeves................................	$10.00
lined...................................	$15.00
Reline..	$30-40 plus fabric
longer length.................................	$40-45 plus fabric
fuller flared longer length..........................	$45 plus fabric
Narrow shoulders................................	$18 & up
lined...............................	$22.50 & up
Narrow lapels...................................	$30.00
narrow only lower section of lapel..............	$20.00
Add interlining.................................	$35 plus fabric
Replace jacket front zipper.......................	$10 plus zipper
Ski jacket pocket zipper................................	$7.50 plus zipper
with vent and buttons (lined).....................	$20.00 & up
with vent and buttons (6-8).........................	$19.00 & up
with vent and buttons (lined).....................	$22.00 & up
new interfacing added.............................	$1.00 extra

Pricing For Creative Sewing

What Is Creative Sewing?

What is creative sewing? Creative Sewing applies to sewing machine artists and crafts persons who are currently creating objects of art with their sewing machines; everything from wearable art to quilts, crafts, stuffed toys and manipulated fabrics. Also included would be covered buttons, earrings, hair bows, purses, draw string bags—you name it.

Saundra Weed—The undisputed guru of creative pricing shares her secrets to success.

Creativity is one of the hardest things to price. It can cause the initial pricing process to be unrealistically high, and prevent the customer from purchasing the art work. Adjustments will need to be made to bring the art work into a realistic, affordable price range. It is not difficult to reconcile *creativity* and *money* without compromising your integrity as an artist. The following questions will help you integrate craftsmanship and creativity to equal **Cash**:

1. Are you an *expert* in your field?
2. What kind of equipment do you own? Is it current?
3. What is your skill level? Is it up-to-date and professional?
4. Are you buying your materials at wholesale or discount prices?
5. In your pricing method, are you allowing for markup and profit margin?
6. Is this an original *Design*, and not a new version of someone else's art work?
7. Does your equipment allow you to produce products easily and professionally?

If the answer is *YES* to all, we can proceed with pricing. If your answer is *NO* to any, you will need to make some adjustments before you begin. Customers are willing to pay for "*creativity*", but they are not willing to pay for poor quality or poor production methods on your part. It is important for you to understand that the experimental piece is not always your big money maker…it is your sample. It is where you first work out the kinks and problems; the design and construction problems as well as the color combinations. Do you get paid for this effort? Eventually, yes! But not always at the time you are creating the piece. Samples can be sold later. But first samples show your skill and expertise and solve construction problems.

Only now, after doing your "homework," can you begin a realistic assessment of the pricing procedure. During the sample-making process, you need to keep a record of time involved to make the sample and the cost of materials used. Although this is not the only formula for pricing, it is one of the simplest and most accurate systems for the home sewer creating a product to sell.

"Quiz"
Name four categories of creative sewing.
Hint: Wearable Art and …

See Answer in paragraph one on this page.

Planning Your Income

One year's income equals— 50 work weeks per year - 5 work days per week - 40 hours per week.

YEAR	WEEK	DAY	HOUR
$100,000	2,000	400	50.00
$50,000	1,000	200	25.00
$25,000	500	100	12.50
$12,500	250	50	6.25
$10,000	200	40	5.00
$5,000	100	20	5.00

Select your desired yearly income, then follow across to determine what you must do to earn it. This is a very easy, visual, way to make your business dream a reality. Now you can see how much energy you need to expend in order to make the kind of income you want. You may need to increase your skill levels, sell more volume, charge higher prices or develop new designs and equipment to boost your income. Choose your *dream* income and follow the line across to figure out how much money you need to generate per week, day, and hour. Can you do it? If not, choose a more realistic goal for now and continue to work toward your dream.

Pricing

Below is a price sheet taken from the book *Creative Sewing As A Business*. This form is used to calculate pricing for creative sewing. The following pages will demonstrate how to use the Home-Based Business Pricing Formula. See the examples on the next two pages: Home-Based Business Pricing Formula, and Reversible Art Vest Example.

CREATIVE SEWING PRICING SHEET

Cost of Materials =	$ _____
Time to Make = _____ hrs. _____ min. =	_____
Hourly Wage = _____ x hours worked =	_____
Overhead = _____	_____
(percentage of home allowed for business)	_____
Profit Margin = _____ (5% to 15%) =	_____
This is the manufacturing total and does = not necessarily represent the retail price	$ _____
Direct Sale (25%)	_____
Retail Sale (Double Wholesale)	_____
Wholesale Price (If you wish to sell wholesale, how low can you go and still make money?)	_____

Pricing

Although this is not the only formula for pricing, it is one of the simplest and most accurate systems for the home sewer, creating a product to sell. As I stated earlier: *"Creativity"* is one of the hardest things to price. Adjustments will need to be made to bring the art work into a realistic, affordable price range. It is not difficult to reconcile *creativity* and *money* without compromising your integrity as an artist.

Retailers will double the price automatically. In many cases, it is the doubling that now causes what the customer *perceives* as an unrealistic sale price. If you, the artist, can sell direct to the consumer, you will be able to add on an additional 25% increase to your price. That 25% is for your creativity for each art piece. If you are relying on a retailer to sell your product, it will take a much longer time to recover your creative investment. The biggest difference between a "Creative Business" and a product business is that the creative business first has to create the product to sell.

How To Calculate Labor For Creative Sewing

The chart below give the formulas needed the calculate pricing. Use the chart as a basis for arriving at pricing for retail, wholesale and manufacturers prices. On the opposite page is a full scale version used to calculate pricing for the art vest in column two.

Home-Based Business Pricing Formula

Definition

Home square footage = A
Workplace square footage = W
Percentage occupied = W ÷ A = P
Cost of Materials = C
Time To Make Garment (hrs) = T
Wages = Wage per hour x T = H
Overhead per month (÷ 4 weeks) = O
Hours Worked in a week = L
Work area usage per hour = O ÷ L = G
Profit Margin = M
Creativity Percentage = B

Formulas

M x [C + H + (T x (G x P)] = Mfg. Price = F
(B x F) + F = Creative Price = E
2 x F = Retail Price
2 x E = Creative Retail Price

Note: Use the definitions and formulas to follow the example for the art vest in column two. You will see pricing for: Manufacture, Creative Manufacture and Retailers price.

Example: Art Vest

Home square Footage = A = 1200 sq. ft
Workplace square footage = W = 120 sq. ft
Cost of Materials = C = $34.26
Time to make Garment = T = 3 hrs
Wages = 12.50/hr x 3 hrs = H = $37.50
Overhead = O = $100/month
Hours Worked in a week = L = 40 hrs
Profit Margin = M = 5%
Creativity Percentage = B = 25%

Manufacturer's Price

M x [C + H + (T x (G x P))]
.05 x [$34.26 + $37.50 + (3 x (2.5 x .1))] = $76.14 = Mfg. Price

Creative Manufacturer's Price

(F x B) = Creative Mfg. Price
($76.14 x .25) + $76.14 = $95.18

Retailers Price

2 x $76.14 = $152.28 = Retail Price
2 x $95.18 = $190.36 = Creative Retail Price

Reversible Art Vest

1. **Cost of Materials**   **$34.26**
   · fabric - 3 yds. @ $6.00 =   18.00
   · thread - 3 @%3.59 =   10.77
   · buttons - 1 pkg. @ $2.50 =   2.50
   · charms - 1 pkg. @ $1.99 =   1.99
   · pearls -5 yds. @ $1.00 =   1.00

2. **Time to Make**   **3 hours**
   · 1/2 hour to cut out
   · 2 1/2 hours to design/sew

3. **Hourly Wage**   **$37.50**
   · $12.50 per hour **x** 3 hours

4. **Overhead (for work area)**   **$0.75**
   · [Rent + Utilities + Phone] per month ! 4 = $400 ! 4 = $100 per week
   · $100 **x** 1O% (percent of house allowed for work area) = $10·
     $10 / 40 hours worked per week = $0.25 per hour for work area
   · %0.25 **x** 3 hours=$0.75

SUBTOTAL: $72.51

5. Profit Margin, 5% $3.62

   ·Subtotal **x** 5% profit margin = $72.51 **x** 5% = $3.62

TOTAL: $76.13

1. Manufacturer's Price = $ 76.50
   At the manufacturer's price, you make labor plus *cost of materials.*

2. 25% Direct Sale = $ 95.13
   At the 25% additional creative price, you get paid for "creativity "

3. Retail Price = $ 154.00
   At the retail price, all you *get is the manufacturer's price; the store gets the other half.*

4. Retail + Creative = % ~92.00
   If you sell to stores and include your creative price, the retailer will still double the price

Turn Scraps Into Cash

One important area often overlooked by a new business is creating additional income or "good will gifts" from the scraps they are throwing away. For seamstresses and quilters the scraps usually take the shape of small pieces of fabric, odds and ends of lace and ribbon, a single button or lace appliqué. The "creative" business owner will turn those scraps into money! Here are some suggestions, even small scraps can be used to make:

- ☑ Covered buttons and earrings
- ☑ Hair bows and scrunchies
- ☑ Makeup or jewelry bags
- ☑ Purses and tote bags
- ☑ Draw string bags
- ☑ Bean bags or sewing weights

All of the above suggestions when made up, could be used as *giveaways*. They become special free "Thank you" gifts to your favorite customers. These "freebies" as we call them in the trade, can also be attached to attractive display cards and sold at art fairs and craft shows for additional income.

No scrap of lace, fabric or beads goes unused in my home, everything is recycled. Saving all those "scraps" has allowed me to reach another one of my dreams. I remodel and reconstruct Vintage Wedding Gowns— I get to use up my "stash" and earn money doing it. One of my 100 goals was to earn money doing what I love to do, and I love beads and lace.

Storing Scraps: The way I store my scraps is to bag them by type: size, color, or kind of fabric. If I don't use them myself I can sell them to someone who can.

Examples Of Scrap To Cash
- ☑ Sell bags of same size fabric squares to quilters.
- ☑ Bags of odd sizes of fabric/trims could be sold to doll makers.
- ☑ Make fabric accessories to be sold at craft shows.
- ☑ Pieces for: quilts; appliqués; vests; soft boxes; album covers; napkins; table runners.

Saundra Weed has a book entitled, *Creative Sewing As A Business.* To order call 800-795-8999 or see featured guest page in this text.

Answer To Quiz
Name four categories of creative sewing.

Wearable art ,quilts, crafts, stuffed toys and manipulated fabrics

Home Décor — Interior Design

One of the hottest fields for sewing for profit is home décor or custom interior design. Sewing professionals have complained that there just aren't any resources available to help them price for profit. In order to satisfy this need I went to the expert—Trenia Bell-Will. Trenia has over 20 years of experience in the design and construction of custom window treatments, interior accessories and slipcovers. She has taught interior design at Radford University and New River Community College. She gives seminars to workroom professionals, and interior designers. Formerly a professional interior designer, she now runs a single person high-end drapery and slipcover workroom. Her window treatment designs have been published by the McCall Pattern Company. Ms. Bell-Will is the expert in the field of home décor and she is extremely knowledgeable when it comes to pricing for profit. I asked Trenia a series of questions that I am sure you will find helpful in your home décor business as you price for profit. Here is what Trenia had to say:

What is your specialty? My field of specialty is in sewing for interiors. I make and install custom window treatments, pillow covers, bed covers, and slipcovers.

What are the pros of sewing for interiors? Once established, the work is steady. The per job compensation is generally high, requiring less than 10 jobs per month. The work (window treatments, slipcovers, etc.) is very visible to friends and relatives, and this results in a high referral rate. Seeing your work as part of a beautiful interior is also very satisfying.

What are the cons of sewing for interiors? The risk incurred by the seamstress can be high, because decorator fabrics generally cost more ($20.00- $200.00) per yard and the amount of yards also can be quite high (10-50 yards). The diversity of sewing requirements and installations means the learning curve is greater. The sewing space required is greater, and a large cutting table is very important. To present a professional product, a serger and a blind stitch hemming machine are also important, added expenses.

What enticed you to go into sewing for interiors? I began as a professional interior designer. After having my children and experiencing some burn out with that career, sewing for interiors as a home based business seemed a logical choice.

Did you have a mentor? No, I did not have a mentor. As an interior designer I was able to observe a wide variety of custom sewn products, and this helped me tremendously. I also learned a great deal by making mistakes, something I don't recommend. As a professional, I now mentor others when they request my help. I think it is important to further the standards of quality, and hope that those I help will in turn help someone else.

How did you learn your craft? I learned from a variety of places. The most important learning tools have been learning by observing how others made things, books, and making my own mistakes, corrections, and improvements. I learn from magazine articles and sewing workroom seminars. I recently joined some online sewing associations, which have also been great sources of information.

In your opinion, what does a sewing entrepreneur need to know before going into business? I think the most important things that someone needs to know is how to generally sew well, to want to improve, and to have a sense of what is excellent sewing. If a person has this as a base, the rest of the knowledge will follow. If they don't know this, they will not be successful.

How do you handle and eliminate price resistance? I handle price resistance with the confidence I have from knowing there is a steady demand for my work. As long as I have a backlog of work, my prices are not too high; however, there are clients that cannot afford my work. As a sole employee of my business, my limited time is what I sell, it will not increase, but the price I charge can increase as long as there is a demand for it. I think it is important to price to your market, if there is a refusal because of price and you have no work, just trying to talk someone into paying is probably not going to be effective. You can upgrade your quality, spend some time making samples to sell from (justify the prices by showing your skill) and work on marketing. Also, you can lower your prices slightly until the work builds, and that way as the work builds so can the prices. I eliminate price resistance by showing the quality of my work; both with samples and photographs of installed jobs. I feel that my backlog of work is also helpful. The backlog reasoning is that if I have this much work, I must be good. I also ask a lot of questions, and give choices when I am selling. I will not do the work for less money; but I will do less work for less money. This establishes me, as the person that will do the best job, so the pricing is almost a formality at the point of sale.

Based on your knowledge and expertise, what advice would you give someone on how to overcome the fear of pricing? My best advice to someone on pricing is to realize that being high in price is not a bad thing, it is an indication of the quality of work you do. Pricing is not a set in stone thing, it can go higher or lower depending on what you need, and what you can ask, not what the customer needs. It is not a compliment when someone says you are inexpensive, it means you are not a good businessperson. It is important to understand you do not need to get every job you price, you only want profitable work.

What are the pricing excuses you've heard people use? The only pricing excuse I can think of is there are some who feel they need to be competitive with factory produced goods. They feel this pricing is too low to be profitable and grumble. This mass merchandise price is low, but the quality is also only acceptable. Custom sewing provides many ways to improve on the products, so the custom pricing can certainly be higher.

How do you establish your pricing guidelines? My pricing guidelines are based loosely on a price of $35.00 per hour. This figure goes up if the fabric has special needs, the treatment is difficult or unusual, the customer is difficult, and how large my work backlog is. The prices go down a bit in slow times, for jobs I really want to do, for clients I like, and steady wholesale customers (decorators, designers).

Do you price from a pattern? I do not price from patterns. Pricing is based on the size of the window or job and the custom product I am making.

What are the pros and cons of flat fee pricing when sewing for interiors? Flat fee pricing gives wholesale customers an easy guideline for pricing a job, but this does not allow for individual job requirements. This may result in more work but is a little iffy on the compensation for the work. Some fabrics and jobs require more or less time.

Below is an extract from Trenia Bell-Will's pricing (see example of a detailed price list at the end of this chapter or to order Home Décor Price List and Forms—see order form at end of this book).

Machine trims, banding	$4.00 per yard
Hand sewn trim	$10.00 per yard
Ruffles	$8.00 per yard
Hand sewn hems, interlining	$30.00-50.00 per width
Prewash, iron slipcover fabric	$35.00 per 8 yards
Installation	$8.00-16.00 per bracket
Pattern, unusual product design charge	$35.00-150.00

What are the pros and cons of pricing by the hour when sewing for interiors? This results in a more secure profit for the seamstress, but leaves the client wondering exactly how much the job will cost them. I feel this is the only way to price when there must be a great deal of client interaction, or it is a remake situation. Remakes or special needs fabrics are so difficult to estimate the sewing time that will be needed and this is the only way I will accept some work.

What are the pros and cons of an integrated pricing system when sewing for interiors? I think the best pricing is a set quoted price based on an estimate of the time required and the difficulty or quality of the sewing. This is a fair way to compensate for the work but also is a secure price for the customer.

Do you charge a consultation fee? My trip charge, measure/fabric estimation charge of $35.00 can be considered a consultation fee. I charge for this because it is generally something that is a service on difficult jobs for designers. Designers are wholesale customers, I give them discounts for taking care of the sale, if they need help on certain jobs it provides me compensation for the additional time I spend.

Do you charge mileage when you go to a client's home? I do not charge mileage provided the job is within my normal range. If the job is some distance away I will charge $35.00 per hour spent traveling.

If a client wants you to go shopping with them, do you charge them for your time and mileage? If someone wants me to shop with them, I also charge a flat $35.00 per hour fee to cover my time and mileage.

Since we know that pricing involves more than just simple math, what other elements affect the pricing structure? Some of the things that will affect my pricing are:

If a client is nice or difficult	If it is a wholesale or retail customer
Their payment history (promptness)	If it is a rush or deadline job
If it contains a special needs fabric	The amount of handiwork required
If it is an unusual or difficult product	The difficulty of the installation
If I have a backlog of work	

How do you market and advertise to get clients? I do no straight advertising. I do, however, promote my work. I think advertising, in the traditional sense, requires there to be a need at the same time someone incidentally finds out you are offering a service. This combination is a difficult thing when your business does not rely on quantity, but the quality of your work. To get new work, I rely on the fabric stores that generously pass out my cards. I make up quality samples for the store at no charge and teach classes for them in return. I ensure repeat customers by doing good work, leaving several cards, and sewing custom labels in my work that have my name and phone number. The purpose of marketing is to ensure that you have a quantity of potential customers to sell and choose jobs from. Pricing can be higher in proportion to the jobs sold and the amount of potential customers. For another business, I have done direct mail post-cards to a very select neighborhood and found that to be effective and inexpensive. A friend has had good success with quick copy color brochures in knob hanger bags. She places them in the neighborhoods where she has current jobs and on the doors of new homes. I would recommend both of these promotions to someone starting out; I will use them if I need to relocate.

How important are layaway, gift-wrapping, Visa, MasterCard, American Express and checks, and discounts to pricing? Lay away, gift-wrap, and credit cards are not things that are an important aspect to my business. As far as discounts are concerned, I do not give discounts to retail customers. I do however give wholesale customers a 10-50% discount off a quoted retail price. The written quote is something they can show their customers, I write it higher or lower depending on what discount they wish to be included, most of the time it is 30%.

Do you feel the image of your business has an impact on how you charge for your goods and services? The term "business image" includes a lot of things. It is the total perception your customers have of you. There are many things that affect this, your personal appearance, what your old customers say about you, examples of your work, your sewing studio appearance, and the business cards and billing sheets you use. I feel that your image is your business, and this impacts on your pricing completely. This does not mean that you need to be in office attire or your studio and business forms need to be the best available. It does mean that you need to act like a business. You do need to dress nicely, use appropriate business forms, and keep your sewing studio neat and efficient. If you use a ducky notepad for billing, greet your clients in pajamas and sew from a corner of the dining room, this impacts your credibility and your ability to build a customer base. The more customers that can be generated, the higher the quality, then the higher the prices you charge can be.

Do you think there is a direct link between being able to get more money for your services in a commercial location versus your home? I feel the best location for a single person sewing business is in a home or another low overhead space. This is not a business that can generate a lot of low cost sales. Sewing for interiors by nature is just a few larger jobs that require quality sewing. A commercial location gives your business visibility and walk in traffic at generally a fairly high overhead cost. Business visibility is better in other locations such as samples in fabric stores and influential customers homes, the walk-in traffic consumes time and interrupts the work, and profit is spent on rent. For a multi-person sewing business the commercial location might be good if someone can be hired to work the door. I don't think storefront prices could be higher because of the location, they may even be lowered by the need to be competitive with quantity outlets. Sewing for interiors has to be a quality, luxury type of service in order for prices and salary to be high. As long as it is a well-run business, location is not important. Another point to consider is most of the time a trip is required to look at the job, measure the windows, and look at what is suitable for the interior. This is when most of the customer contact/sale is made, not in my sewing studio. Wholesale customers also rarely come to my studio; I pick up and deliver to them.

How do you price for retail establishments and for consignment? I price my wholesale quotes with a discount built in, usually 30%. I do not sell anything on consignment.

How do you find wholesale establishments to sell to and what criteria do you use to select them? The wholesale for interiors sewing is primarily done for interior decorators and designers. To find them, look in the phone book and call for an appointment to introduce your business and show samples of your work. Your samples should have design details that are interesting; good hand sewing, and overall be neat in appearance. Samples have two uses, they can teach you how to make an item and provide a selling tool. Selecting the designers you want to work for can be a little tricky. Select them on the basis of an overall relationship, can you discuss things well with them, are they prompt with payments, provide enough yards, give good work orders, and are they reasonable in their requests? Another working relationship that is good to discuss here is the interior designer compensated by a commission? If an interior designer does not offer custom window treatments, then a commission agreement can be set up to benefit both. Most often the designer will be working at a high-end furniture store and will call the workroom in to complete the job. The designer and seamstress will work together, the job labor and fabrics are sold by the workroom at retail pricing. When the job is completed the designer receives a percentage, usually 10%. These arrangements result in a steady flow of work at higher prices but also benefits the designer by adding on to the sale, increasing income, and completing the room.

Do you hire employees or subcontract? If so, how do you calculate the percentage of profit to give? My work is specialized. The studio, while adequate for a single person, is not large. For these reasons I do not have any employees working for me most of the time. Occasionally I will have a sewing friend help on larger jobs, we trade time (I help her install window treatments) or I will pay a flat hourly rate, not a percentage of the job. I will subcontract some things to a larger factory type workroom. Mostly the things I send out are quilted bedspreads, and pinch pleat draperies. The workroom has equipment that allows them to do these things reasonably well at a much lower cost than I require. I will mark up their cost 50 % or so depending on the job.

Do you think that when you take a sewing course, it allows you to charge more for your new knowledge and expertise? I don't think just because I have taken a class or learned something new I can charge more for my products. There are, however, real benefits to learning. I am always searching for sewing techniques that will improve the time it takes to make something; small things can make a significant difference. It is just not realistic to think that at some point you will suddenly sew faster, you have to sew smarter. If it takes less time to make something, your per hour compensation is larger. Another benefit to classes and learning is that this gives me a higher standard of quality or a design detail that other workrooms don't know. If I have a reputation for special work that other workrooms can't do or can't do well, then my pricing on special items can be higher. But this reasoning is more general; I can't take a shade class and charge 30% more for shades. I can charge 30% more if my shades are better quality or the design details are wonderful.

So many sewing professionals feel they can only get business in their small sphere of influence. How would you advise them to open their thinking to a larger geographical area? I think a custom sewing for interiors business requires a fairly specialized luxury market, one that is not necessarily a personal circle of friends, family and acquaintances. You can learn your craft within this circle though; they will not be so hard on you if you make errors. Then, once you have jobs to your credit, I recommend marketing to interior designers, neighborhoods of larger exclusive homes, and decorative fabric stores. If you can find these near you, good, if not, it is worthwhile to go to where they are. If you live in a smaller town, but are near a city, consider making the commute. I do most of my work about an hour's drive away, where the demand for custom work is greater and the prices I can charge are also higher. I go into the city to pick up and deliver work about every ten days, and it's not a hardship at all.

Can you tell us about your sewing studio? I work in the lower level of a split-level house; the room would normally be used as a recreation room. It has good windows, natural light, is about 20' X 20', and is carpeted. I have two cutting/ironing tables, one is 4' X 8' one is 3' X 4'.5". The tables can be moved together to create a larger surface. A 60" X 120" table would be my choice but the room will not hold that size. I have a long table for the serger and standard machine, and a smaller table for the blind stitch hemmer. A rolling table expands the machine table surface when I need it. I also have an electric rotary cutter, storage shelf, fabric bolt storage, treadmill, and office area.

What made you decide on this type of layout and design? Do you think it has enhanced your production, ultimately increasing your profit margin? There is no great thought put into this plan; it has evolved as I have added equipment, as the need has presented itself. A U-shape arrangement seems to be the most useful for me; it limits the amount of traffic through my workspace by my family. I think the arrangement makes it pleasant to work, and I have a nice view of the yard from the tables. I don't know if the layout and design of my sewing studio has any significant influence on my production or not. This plan could be improved, it is a make do arrangement using some of what I had from a sewing room in a previous house that was much smaller.

Do you sell fabric and notions to your customers? I do not sell fabrics and notions to my customers. I will provide linings and hardware for retail jobs on a reimbursement basis only. My wholesale customers provide linings, fabric and hardware for their jobs. A large proportion of my work comes from fabric store referrals; it is a good arrangement for me since I find selling fabrics difficult. Many of my sewing friends sell fabric, but for me the time spent, low volume, costs, and the larger store's lower pricing made it not worthwhile. I find that my higher labor cost is not a problem and my retail customers like making their own deal on fabrics.

Do you buy fabric and notions in bulk from a manufacturer or wholesaler? I purchase lining fabric and notions in bulk at considerable savings. Some of the things I buy in quantity are slipcover zippers, cords, shade rings, hardware, machine needles, buckram, polyfill and interlinings.

How did you find them? I found my sources from ads in trade and sewing magazines, from sewing workroom shows, and from networking with sewing friends.

How did you negotiate the margins with them? I have not negotiated with my suppliers. I feel the pricing is fair for the quantity I purchase.

How do you calculate your markup to sell to customers? I do not mark up products to sell to my customers, the amounts involved are small, and it is difficult to mark up and not overcharge as compared to other larger retail outlets. I find that my higher labor price is not objectionable, but if I am high in price on an easily shopped drapery rod it can be a problem.

Do you teach sewing? What courses do you teach? How do you charge for lessons? Do you give group discounts? Yes, I teach sewing for interiors classes. I teach full day and half day seminars at a fabric store. The prices vary from $15.00 to $60.00 per class depending on the subject. I teach window treatments, pillows, slipcover fitting, and decorating. I also have taken single students for day classes at $150.00 per day. The subject of group discounts has not been asked of me so I have not considered it. If a discount were requested, I would consider it based on the number of students and the material being taught. All day single student classes have been about setting up a sewing business or pin fitting slipcovers. I am hoping to expand my teaching and writing for interiors. I am exploring teaching professional sewing for interiors classes online. I am also in the planning stages of a pattern company that will specialize in styles for interiors.

Below is a sample of Trenia's old quotation forms. She now uses customized forms for pricing her projects. Also, are two pictures of Trenia's most recent projects.

Custom Interiors by Trenia Bell-Will

Designs by Trenia Bell-Will

Trenia has designed a number of patterns for McCalls Pattern Company. On the next page are examples of two of her patterns.

Note: Trenia has designed 38 forms for interior designers, sewing workrooms, fabricators, and other trade professionals. A detailed list follows in this chapter. To order these forms, see order blank at the end of this text.

**Interior Design by Trenia Bell-Will, ASID
Photograph Courtesy Of The McCall Pattern Company**

Forms For Custom Interiors by Trenia Bell-Will

Business Organization

1. Wholesale client information
2. Retail client information
3. Job estimate worksheet
4. Quotation
5. Client purchase contract
6. Terms and conditions
7. Credit application
8. Sales tax exemption
9. Job record of charges, payments, order tracking

10. Purchase order
11. Purchase order record
12. Job tag
13. Job time record, supplies cost, profit statement
14. Expenses spreadsheet
15. Income spreadsheet
16. Invoices worksheet
17. Jobs in progress worksheet
18. Monthly financial summary

Measure and Design

19. Window measures
20. Bed measures
21. Upholstery, slipcover measures
22. Wallpaper measures
23. Floor covering measures
24. Window design drawing
25. Bedcover design drawing
26. Chair design drawing

To order these forms, please see order blank at the end of this book.

Custom Work Orders

27. General custom work order
28. Drapery, curtain work order
29. Shade work order
30. Top treatment work order
31. Swag work order
32. Bedcover work order
33. Pillow work order
34. Table skirt work order
35. Upholstery, slipcover work order
36. Window treatment installation work order
37. Wall finish work order
38. Floor cover work order

Sample Of A Form Designed by Trenia Bell-Will

Accessory Order Form   Trenia Bell-Will   703-639-6080

Name _____   Date _____

Street _____   Designer _____

City _____   Company _____

Phone (H) _____ (W) _____   Phone _____

Quan	Style	Description	Size	D/P	Fabric	Each	Extended

Fit _____   Tax _____

By _____   Total _____

Accepted _____   Deposit _____

                                              Bal. Due _____

Home Décor Price List

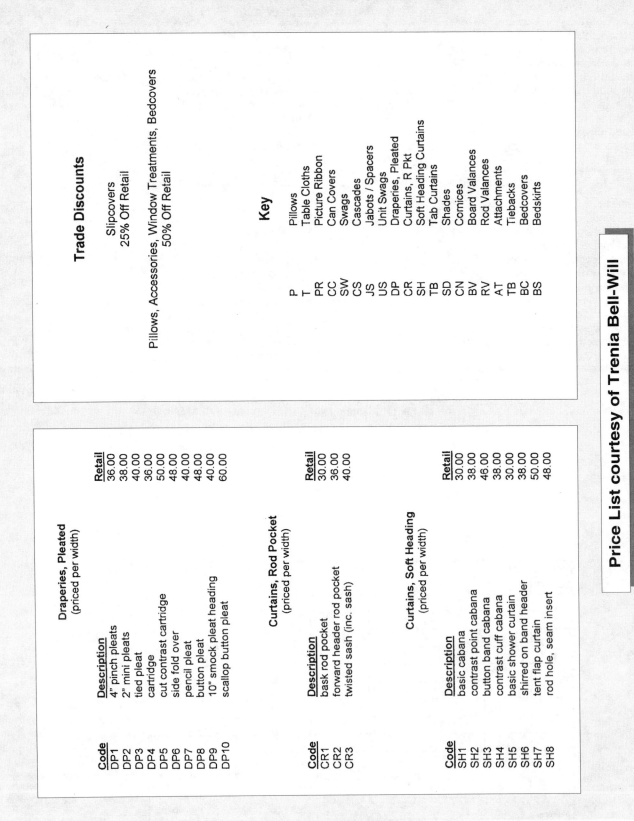

Trade Discounts

Slipcovers
25% Off Retail

Pillows, Accessories, Window Treatments, Bedcovers
50% Off Retail

Key

P	Pillows
T	Table Cloths
PR	Picture Ribbon
CC	Can Covers
SW	Swags
CS	Cascades
JS	Jabots / Spacers
US	Unit Swags
DP	Draperies, Pleated
CR	Curtains, R Pkt
SH	Soft Heading Curtains
TB	Tab Curtains
SD	Shades
CN	Cornices
BV	Board Valances
RV	Rod Valances
AT	Attachments
TB	Tiebacks
BC	Bedcovers
BS	Bedskirts

Draperies, Pleated
(priced per width)

Code	Description	Retail
DP1	4" pinch pleats	36.00
DP2	2" mini pleats	38.00
DP3	tied pleat	40.00
DP4	cartridge	36.00
DP5	cut contrast cartridge	50.00
DP6	side fold over	48.00
DP7	pencil pleat	40.00
DP8	button pleat	48.00
DP9	10" smock pleat heading	40.00
DP10	scallop button pleat	60.00

Curtains, Rod Pocket
(priced per width)

Code	Description	Retail
CR1	bask rod pocket	30.00
CR2	forward header rod pocket	36.00
CR3	twisted sash (inc. sash)	40.00

Curtains, Soft Heading
(priced per width)

Code	Description	Retail
SH1	basic cabana	30.00
SH2	contrast point cabana	38.00
SH3	button band cabana	46.00
SH4	contrast cuff cabana	38.00
SH5	basic shower curtain	30.00
SH6	shirred on band header	38.00
SH7	tent flap curtain	50.00
SH8	rod hole, seam insert	48.00

Price List courtesy of Trenia Bell-Will

Home Décor Price List

Swags
(priced per each)

Code	Description	Retail
SW1	standard 5 pleat swag	60.00
SW2	overlay swag, 2-3 pleat	50.00
SW3	gathered swag	56.00
SW4	pinch corner swag	70.00
SW5	small panel swag w/ cascade	70.00
SW6	asymmetric swag	70.00

Cascades
(priced per pair)

Code	Description	Retail
CW1	standard step fold cascade	68.00
CW2	1/2 width cascade (short)	44.00
CW3	extra long	80.00
CW4	gathered cascade	60.00
CW5	stack fold cascade	68.00
CW6	drapery panel cascade	48.00 (wom)
CW7	1/2 width cascade 1 1/2" header add	20.00
CW8	fill cascade 2" header add	28.00

Jabots / Stackers
(priced per each)

Code	Description	Retail
JS1	step fold jabot	34.00
JS2	gathered jabots	30.00
JS3	cone pleated	38.00

Unit Swags
(priced per linear foot)

Code	Description	Retail
US1	Lucas swag	36.00
US2	pull up swag	24.00
US3	Victoria swag valance	36.00
US4	pinch pleat rod swag	30.00
US5	Windsor	38.00

Curtains, Tab
(priced per width)

Code	Description	Retail
TB1	basic tab curtain	36.00
TB2	tie tabs	36.00
TB3	contrast twisted tab and inset	38.00
TB4	tab and tab inset hem	58.00

Shades
(priced per sq. foot)

Code	Description	Retail
SD1	basic Roman	16.00
SD2	fan hem Roman	16.00
SD3	soft fold Roman	18.00
SD4	stitched fold Roman	18.00
SD5	contrast point hem option	+10.00
SD6	mini valance	6.00 ft
SD7	basic pleated balloon	16.00
SD8	shirr tape balloon	16.00
SD9	contrast pleat balloon	20.00

Cornices
(priced per linear foot)

Code	Description	Retail
CN1	straight, single welt	30.00
CN2	bottom shaped, single welt	36.00
CN3	dynamic pleated	40.00
CN4	straight / contrast verticle welts	34.00
CN5	1/2 cornices, shaped	40.00
CN6	2 side shaped, welted	48.00

Price List courtesy of Trenia Bell-Will

Home Décor Price List

Board Valances
(priced per linear foot)

Code	Description	Retail
BV1	simple pleated, straight hem	26.00
BV2	simple pleated, shaped hem	30.00
BV3	complex pleated, straight hem	32.00
BV4	complex pleated, shaped hem	40.00
BV5	shirred, straight hem	26.00
BV6	shirred, shaped hem	28.00
BV7	shirring taped with header	30.00
BV8	plain, corner pleat	20.00
BV9	plain, saw tooth hem	34.00
BV10	overlapping diamond	30.00
BV11	V pleat and tack	38.00
BV12	bell and scallop	34 lf.

Rod Valances
(priced per width)

Code	Description	Retail
RV1	tied pleats	40.00
RV2	rod pocket, straight hem	26.00
RV3	rod pocket, shaped hem	28.00
RV4	stationary cloud valance	40.00

Attachments
(priced per each)

Code	Description	Retail
AT1	single rosettes	20.00
AT2	double rosette	28.00
AT3	oval rosette	24.00
AT4	bunchie	26.00
AT5	bow, small	20.00
AT6	bow, large	26.00
AT7	4 sided bow	26.00
AT8	rose w/ leaves	28.00
AT9	sash	20.00

Tiebacks
(priced per pair)

Code	Description	Retail
TB1	straight tiebacks	32.00
TB2	ring and cord tieback	28.00
TB3	oversized	40.00

Bedcovers
(priced per each)

Code	Description	Retail
BC1	unlined / bound coverlet	80.00
BC2	lined coverlet	140.00
BC3	welt edge duvet	140.00
BC4	ruffle duvet	140.00
BC5	cord and ruffle duvet	160.00
BC6	basic flange duvet	120.00
BC7	double flange duvet	140.00
BC8	contrast flange	160.00
BC9	flange / button band	170.00

Bedskirts
(priced per each)

Code	Description	Retail
BS1	basic pleated bedskirt	120.00
BS2	gathered bedskirt	140.00
BS3	double pleated bedskirt	140.00
BS4	deluxe bedskirt	180.00

Shams
see pillow group prices

Price List courtesy of Trenia Bell-Will

Home Décor Price List

Other Charges

Code	Description	Retail
OC1	lining, roc lon	5.00 yd
OC2	interlining	by quote
OC3	bay board cut charge	40.00
OC4	arch board cut charge	30.00
OC5	two level board	40.00
OC6	apply matching trim	10.00 yd
OC7	apply hand trim / ruffles	20.00 yd

Installation

Code	Description	Retail
I1	Trip Charge Minimum	10.00
I2	std. rod per bracket	6.00
I3	rod treatment per wom	16.00
I4	traverse rod per bracket	16.00
	board treatments per bracket	
	(brackets placed every 24-30")	

Curtain Rods

Code	Description	Retail
R1	curtain rod, 28-48"	5.00
R2	curtain rod, 48-86"	8.00
R3	traverse rod, 30-48"	21.00
R4	traverse rod, 48-86"	32.00
R5	traverse rod, 66-120"	36.00
R6	traverse rod, 86-150"	41.00
R7	2 1/2" rod, 28-48"	13.40
R8	2 1/2" rod, 48-86"	20.00

Decorative Pillows

Group A

to 14"	16.00	24-26" 22.00
16-18"	18.00	Shams 30.00
20-22"	20.00	

PA1	plain edge, zipper
PA2	flap over, one button close
PA3	flange edge, sew close

Group B

to 14"	24.00	24-26" 36.00
16-18"	28.00	Shams 50.00
20-22"	32.00	

PB1	med cord edge, zipper
PB2	med cord edge, invisible close
PB3	flange edge, zipper
PB4	single ruffle, zipper
PB5	neckroll, tie close

Group C

to 14"	32.00	24-26" 44.00
16-18"	36.00	Shams 65.00
20-22"	40.00	

PC1	cord edge, Turkish corner, zipper
PC2	double ruffle, zipper
PC3	single ruffle, cord, zipper
PC4	single flange padded, zipper
PC5	jumbo cord, zipper
PC6	neckroll, cord edge, covered button end
PC7	Turkish corners buttoned, plain edge
PC8	4 layer buttoned, one size, 9x12
PC10	petal edge, zipper
PC11	point edge, zipper
PC12	pleated ruffle, cord, zipper

Price List courtesy of Trenia Bell-Will

Home Décor Price List

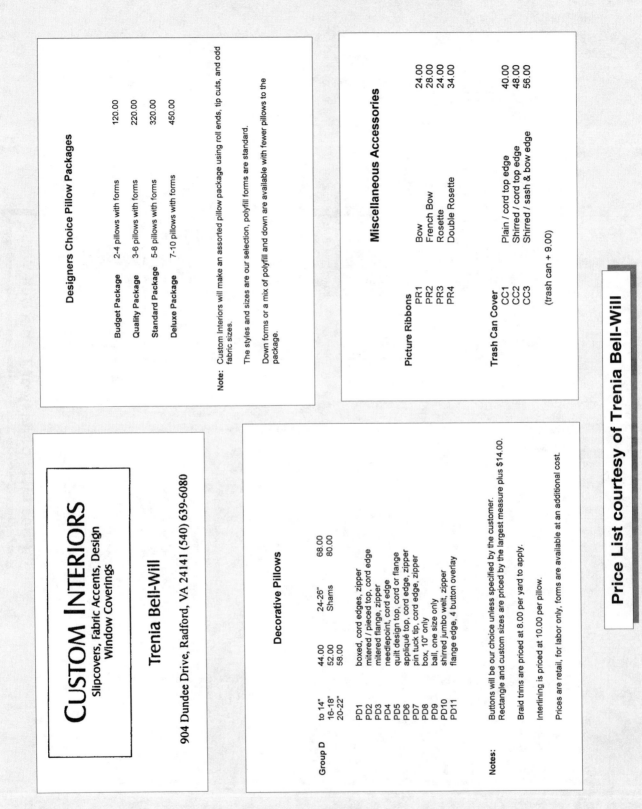

CUSTOM INTERIORS
Slipcovers, Fabric Accents, Design
Window Coverings

Trenia Bell-Will

904 Dundee Drive, Radford, VA 24141 (540) 639-6080

Designers Choice Pillow Packages

Budget Package	2-4 pillows with forms	120.00
Quality Package	3-6 pillows with forms	220.00
Standard Package	5-8 pillows with forms	320.00
Deluxe Package	7-10 pillows with forms	450.00

Note: Custom Interiors will make an assorted pillow package using roll ends, tip cuts, and odd fabric sizes.

The styles and sizes are our selection, polyfill forms are standard.

Down forms or a mix of polyfill and down are available with fewer pillows to the package.

Miscellaneous Accessories

Picture Ribbons

PR1	Bow	24.00
PR2	French Bow	28.00
PR3	Rosette	24.00
PR4	Double Rosette	34.00

Trash Can Cover

CC1	Plain / cord top edge	40.00
CC2	Shirred / cord top edge	48.00
CC3	Shirred / sash & bow edge	56.00

(trash can + 9.00)

Decorative Pillows

Group D			
	to 14"		44.00
	16-18"		52.00
	20-22"		58.00
	24-26"		68.00
	Shams		80.00

PD1	boxed, cord edges, zipper
PD2	mitered / pieced top, cord edge
PD3	mitered flange, zipper
PD4	needlepoint, cord edge
PD5	quilt design top, cord or flange
PD6	appliqué top, cord edge, zipper
PD7	pin tuck tip, cord edge, zipper
PD8	box, 10" only
PD9	ball, one size only
PD10	shirred jumbo welt, zipper
PD11	flange edge, 4 button overlay

Notes: Buttons will be our choice unless specified by the customer.
Rectangle and custom sizes are priced by the largest measure plus $14.00.

Braid trims are priced at 8.00 per yard to apply.

Interlining is priced at 10.00 per pillow.

Prices are retail, for labor only, forms are available at an additional cost.

Price List courtesy of Trenia Bell-Will

Home Décor Price List

Price List courtesy of Trenia Bell-Will

Pillow Forms

Size	Down and Feather	Polyfill
6 x 12 Neckroll	20.00	15.00
12 x 12	14.00	7.00
14 x 14	19.00	9.00
16 x 16	22.00	11.00
18 x 18	29.00	12.00
20 x 20	38.00	14.00
22 x 22	50.00	16.00
24 x 24	59.00	19.00
26 x 26	79.00	24.00

Bed Pillows

Size	Down and Feather	Polyfill
Standard	59.00	18.00
Queen	49.00	24.00
King	39.00	29.00

Duvet Comforters

Size	Down and Feather	Polyfill	Budget Polyfill
Twin	219.00	129.00	69.00
Full / Queen	259.00	189.00	89.00
King	299.00	259.00	129.00

Table Cloths

Group A

to 50"	48.00
50-104"	72.00

TA1   plain hem

Group B

to 50"	68.00
50-104"	86.00

TB1   medium cord hem
TB2   1 1/2" banded hem
TB3   four bow pull up

Group C

to 50"	82.00
50-104"	120.00

TC1   four section mitered
TC2   cord at table edge, pleated
TC3   cord at table edge, shirred
TC4   shirred jumbo welt hem

Note: Lined and unlined are labor priced the same, lining must be supplied or it will be charged at 5.00 yd.

Home Décor Price List

SLIPCOVER YARDS

80 - 90", 6 cushion sofa	18 - 22 Yards
60 - 79", 4 cushion loveseat	16 - 20 Yards
Large, 2 cushion chair	8 - 10 Yards
Small, 1 cushion chair	6 - 8 Yards
Wing Chair, skirted	8 - 10 Yards
Ottoman, skirted	3 - 4 Yards
Dining Chair, armless	4 - 5 Yards

For more accurate yardage information please ask an amount. Generally slipcovers require approximately 10 - 20% more fabric than upholstery.

For a snug fit do not prewash fabrics. Wash cover and put on furniture damp for a shrink to fit cover.

RECOMMENDED FABRICS
Sailcloth, Heavier Cottons, Linen, Ticking, Cotton Damasks, Twill

NOT ACCEPTABLE
Lightweight or loose weave fabrics, moire, silk, tapestry, sheets, upholstery weights

FURNITURE STYLES NOT SUITABLE
Double pillow backs, tufted backs, semi attached backs, recliners, leather or vinyl covered furniture.

TRENIA BELL-WILL
904 DUNDEE DRIVE
RADFORD, VIRGINIA 24141

1995 SLIPCOVER ORDER FORM   TRENIA BELL-WILL   703-639-6080

Name _____
Street _____
City _____
Phone (H) _____ (W) _____

Date _____
Designer _____
Company _____
Phone _____

Prices are base prices. Add to base the number of cushions X price per cushion. A single long cushion is priced as 2 cushions.

QUAN	ITEM	STD WELT PRICE	SIMP NO WELT PRICE	EXTENDED
	Sofa	125.00	105.00	
	Loveseat	105.00	85.00	
	Chair	85.00	65.00	
	Wing Chair	95.00	80.00	
	Armless Chair	55.00	45.00	
	Ottoman	50.00	40.00	
	DR Chair Skirt	25.00	20.00	
	Cushion/Ea	45.00	40.00	

QUAN	OPTION	PRICE	EXTENDED
	Button Placket Close	20.00 + 3.00 per button for self covered	
	Tie Close	10.00 pr, size:	
	Cluster Pleat Skirt	Chair 25.00 Loveseat 40.00	
	Box Pleat Skirt	Sofa 55.00	
	Shirred Skirt	Chair 35.00 Loveseat 50.00	
	Sm. Box. Pleat Skirt	Sofa 65.00	
	3½" Skirt Bows	30.00 Pair	
	Braid, Fringe or Contrast Band	4.50 Yard	
	Pleated Boxing	25.00 Per Cushion	
	Shirred Boxing		
	½" Bias Flange Edge	25% Upcharge	
	Prewash/Iron	25.00 Per 6 yard length	

FABRIC _____

	STANDARD	OVERSIZE	
FIT:			TAX ___
BY:			TOTAL ___
ACCEPTED:			DEPOSIT ___
			BAL DUE ___

Price List courtesy of Trenia Bell-Will

9 Sewing for the Bride — How to Make a Profit

Part One

Susan is the author of *Bridal Couture* and a featured writer for *Threads, Sew News, and Home Expressions Magazine*. Susan is a consummate instructor, she founded *The Bridal Sewing School* in 1993. As a designer, Susan's bridal gowns are priceless. Susan was also the former chair for Professional Association of Custom Clothiers. We asked Susan to share her secrets to success and her pricing methods. Susan gives detailed examples of her pricing at the end of the Q & A's. The following are responses to the many questions we posed to Susan:

What is your field of specialty? Couture bridal and evening wear.

What are some of the advantages related to your field of specialty? People are willing to pay more for a special garment; the psychological and financial rewards can be considerable. The disadvantages are that projects are large in scope, and there is considerable emotional pressure surrounding the entire event.

What enticed you to sew bridal and evening wear? I like detail-oriented work. I like the fact that every gown is different, I get to work with beautiful fabrics, and I like a challenge.

Did you have a mentor? Olga Holzmueller, at the couture salon Chez Cez et Bez, where I trained in New York. Her work is still the standard against which I measure my own.

How did you learn your craft? At Cez et Bez, and then on my own, by reading, observing, studying, and experimenting

What does one need to know prior to going into this business? A full knowledge of textiles, fitting, visual design, must be up-to-date on fashion, must be able to sketch, must have a full knowledge of garment engineering and construction.

How do you handle price resistance? I realize that not everyone is my client—and that although a certain price may be more than someone wants to pay, it is not more than my work is worth!

How do you eliminate price resistance? I screen clients carefully; I show strong evidence of competence and value for the money (my portfolio, my book, sample gowns, clients' gowns-in-progress), and my own level of confidence.

Any advice on fearless pricing? All the technical pieces must be in place? You must solidly know your craft and feel confident with your knowledge. Education and the confidence that follows are the keys.

What are some of the most common pricing excuses? "I can't find people in my area to pay me what I'm worth." "Nobody around here charges that"

What is the key to effective pricing? Your prices must, to some extent, be in line with what the market will bear. I compare, price-wise, to upper and high-end bridal ready-to-wear.

Do you price from a pattern? I always make my own patterns, or adapt a commercial pattern to my design. My gowns start at a certain price, which includes everything.

Do you have a pricing formula? I estimate fabric costs; by now, I know roughly what they will be, and I estimate the work involved. I know what will be straightforward, what will be time-consuming, what will be hard or tricky, and I factor it all in. Wedding gowns typically take between 40 and 100 hours of work. My blanket price has padding built in. I know there are always extras, and I want to feel there's room in the budget to allow me to do what I want to, without resentment.

Do you charge a fee for mileage? It is included in the overall price. I don't go to clients' homes, and I seldom go shopping with them. If I do, it's included in my overall price. If however, I charged by the hour, I would include all of that.

What do you do if the bride gains or looses weight before the project is due? I always ask her if her weight is stable; or if she has a tendency to gain or lose. I may leave the center back seam, for example, as late as possible if I feel that varying weight might be a problem.

Do you give a discount for the bridesmaids? I doubt I would anyway; bridesmaids are too much work for too little money.

What is your opinion of charging by the hour? Although I don't price this way, it is the most exact method, and a wonderful way of educating yourself as to how long things actually take. Personally, I find keeping my eye on the clock to be nerve-wracking. If I were doing alterations, though, I would certainly charge strictly by the hour.

Do you charge a consultation fee? No, but if I saw more potential clients I would, and then I'd apply it to the price of the gown.

Pricing is more than simple math, what other elements are involved? Reputation, the level of your work, your dependability. (Do you stick to appointments, is the work always ready when you say it will be, etc.)

How important is advertising to pricing? Referrals and word of mouth are the best. Without knowledge of your work and reputation, etc., an unqualified price is difficult to justify.

How do you market and advertise your business? With other professionals: wedding planners, photographers, caterers, country club managers, bridal fairs, etc.

How important are the following to pricing?
a. Gift wrapping: I always package a gown beautifully in a gown bag with decorated hanger and lots of pale pink tissue paper. Headpieces are packaged in a decorated hatbox (a silk rose on the lid, for example) with lots of tissue paper *b. Discounts?* No.

Does the image of your business have any impact on how you charge for your goods and services? Of course; I try to present as elegant and sophisticated an image as I can; I am in the fashion business, after all, and I need to look as if I am.

Do you think there is a direct link between being able to charge more money for your services in a commercial location versus your home? I don't think being a home-based business is a drawback. I make the atmosphere professional and elegant. I need to gain the client's confidence, and my surroundings contribute to the image I am trying to convey.

Does taking sewing courses allow you to charge more for your knowledge and expertise? Absolutely. I wish more sewers realized the very tangible value of continuing education. *Do you teach sewing?* I teach couture sewing seminars. I don't give private lessons.

So many sewing pros feel they can only get business in their small sphere of influence. How would you advise them to open their thinking to a larger geographical area? Know that people will travel for quality, especially brides for a once-in-a-lifetime experience.

Can you tell us about your sewing studio? Surprisingly modest! A Bernina, a back-up Bernina (no serger), a Europro iron, a regular dry iron, mannequins, a bookcase of sewing books, worktables, my favorite fashion photos on the wall, lots of good natural light, and a beautiful view. I don't see clients in my studio, though; that is my inner sanctum. I see them in another area in my house, which is more like a small salon. There's a sofa, a large three-fold mirror, my Ikat textile collection on the walls, beautiful Oriental rugs (my husband's business, fortunately!), antique furniture, potpourri to scent the air. I don't particularly want clients to be aware of the behind-the-scenes work. They see the garment in stages, but not what I do to get it there.

Do you sell fabrics and notions to your clients? Those are included in the price; the better I can do on the fabrics and notions, the more profit to me.

Do you buy fabrics and notions in bulk? I stock very little, only silk organza underlining and silk lining; everything else is bought specifically for each project.

Susan Khalje's Pricing Structure

Pricing: Wedding Ensemble

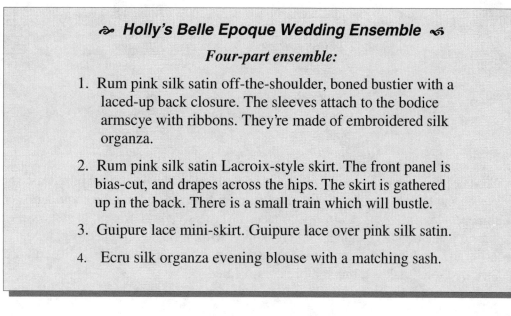

❧ Holly's Belle Epoque Wedding Ensemble ❧

Four-part ensemble:

1. Rum pink silk satin off-the-shoulder, boned bustier with a laced-up back closure. The sleeves attach to the bodice armscye with ribbons. They're made of embroidered silk organza.

2. Rum pink silk satin Lacroix-style skirt. The front panel is bias-cut, and drapes across the hips. The skirt is gathered up in the back. There is a small train which will bustle.

3. Guipure lace mini-skirt. Guipure lace over pink silk satin.

4. Ecru silk organza evening blouse with a matching sash.

Pricing Without Fear

Susan Khalje's Pricing Structure Continued

Pricing Structure For Holly's Belle Epoque Wedding Ensemble		
Pricing Structure: Based on $35 per hour		
Fabric cost	$1,000	
Trip to NYC for fabric	10 hours	$350
Labor	70 hours	$2,450
Fittings	20 hours	$700
Grand Total: Fabric + Labor cost		**$4,500**

Pricing: Mother-of-the-Bride

❧ Janet's Mother-of-the-Bride Ensemble ❧

1. Floor-length silk chiffon gown with a square neckline, cap sleeves, princess seams.

2. Matching jacket with silk charmeuse bands around the jewel neckline, down the center front, and along the bottom edges of the sleeves.

The fabric is a very heavy, all-over glass beaded and sequined silk chiffon. It is underlined with silk crepe, and lined with silk crepe de chine.

Janet's Mother-of-the-Bride Ensemble		
Pricing Structure: Based on $35 dollars per hour		
Fabric cost		$900
Labor	70 hours	$2,450
Fittings	10 hours	$350
Grand Total: Fabric + Labor cost		**$3,700**

To order Susan Khalje's book: ***Bridal Couture***, see "Featured Guest" page.
Send Susan your bridal questions at www.collinspub.com.

Note: I no longer actually "time" jobs. I know roughly what the fabric costs will be, and how much time will be needed. For example, in Holly's gown, nothing is particularly laborious, there's just a lot to do. Perfecting the bodice muslin (it's off-the-shoulder but rests just on the shoulders) required some work, and engineering the center back closure (it laces up) is also a little tricky. In Janet's gown, the weight of the fabric is the biggest element to be reckoned with; it makes engineering, layout, cutting, handling, underlining, stitching, etc., more time-consuming. It's not a particularly difficult dress, but dealing with a tricky fabric makes it much more complicated.

Part Two

Are There Other Pricing Methods That Can Be Used?

Susan's pricing method works effectively for her business. She is able to garner a profit, and she knows her ultimate consumer and what influences them to spend their discretionary dollars with her. But the question still remains: Are there other pricing methods that can be utilized when sewing for the bride or sewing special occasion? The answer is yes, The Integrated Pricing method is excellent (see example in this chapter). You should also review the chapter entitled *Pricing Methods 101*. Study each method: the Flat Fee, By The Hour and The Integrated Pricing method. Examine how to use these pricing methods effectively. More importantly, determine if they can be incorporated into your business. The following is an overview of the integrated pricing method. For more details see chapter four.

Sewing For The Bride Using The Integrated Pricing Method

Bridal gowns have so many intricate details, hand beading, lace appliqués and millions of buttons. The integrated pricing method allows you to charge for the base labor plus all the detailed work that goes into the gown. Knowledge of your production time is your single greatest asset. A time and motion study will help you arrive at those figures. You also need to have a figure to multiply your production time by, better known as the base hourly or base labor rate. There is a specific formula used to obtain the base hourly rate called the pricing formula. The charts listed below will demonstrate how to achieve this goal.

Pricing Formula	Exercise Component Values	Example
There are "3" Components Overhead expense Hours committed Desired salary	1) Overhead expense - $800 2) Hours committed – 160 per month 3) Desired salary- $5,000 $$\frac{\text{Overhead expenses + desired salary}}{\text{Divided by hours committed}} = \text{base hourly rate}$$	$$\frac{\$800 + \$5,000}{160 \text{ hrs}}$$ Formula Set up

How To Calculate The Base Hourly Rate	

Salary + Overhead
 	
1) $5,000
 	
    + 800
    ―――
    $5,800
	2) $5,800 Divided by 160 hrs. = $36.25
	
	3) Round up to $37 dollars
	
	The $37 dollars is your base hourly rate

Learning Your Production Time

To formulate a price list you must have knowledge of how long it takes you to complete a project or task—your production time. Once you have your base hourly rate and all the figures for your production time, you can make a price list.

You will need to have time frames for making a basic gown as well as all the small labor intensive details, such as hand beading, lace appliqués, sequins, buttons, and so on. The method most widely used in business to determine production time is known as a Time and Motion Study. It is not difficult to accomplish, however, it does require some of your precious time.

Time and Motion Study

1. You will need the following to perform the study and make your price list:
2. Project and Task List*
3. Time and Motion Chart*
4. Price List Worksheet*
5. Watch or Clock with second hand
6. Preferably someone to time you
7. Base hourly rate

*These are forms available in the complete set of forms and forms on computer disk.

To perform the time and motion study, you will need to have the forms listed above with an asterisk. On your project and task list you will have all the items listed that you wish to get production times for. You will take each project or task from your list and use the time and motion chart to perform the study. For example, the first item might be hand beading the bodice front. You would start timing yourself the moment you started any work on the bodice. Stop when you take a break and record the time you worked on the bodice. Resume your study after the break and record any additional time spent on the bodice. This process continues until you complete the project or task. In order to keep the study pure, you must stop tracking time when you take breaks or have any interruptions.

After you complete all the items on your project and task list, you will transfer these values to the price list worksheet. Let's say the bodice you worked on took 7 hours; your first line item would be the bodice. Using the base hourly rate obtained from the pricing formula in our previous example, you would multiply your production time by that figure.

Base hourly rate:	$ 37.00
Production time (hand beaded bodice):	x 7
Base Labor Rate	$259.00

Calculating Miscellaneous Items

To maintain structure, and your sanity, you will have to employ methods that allow you to come up with different scenarios regarding pricing your miscellaneous items. For example, you want to price out the top quarter of the bodice front for beading. This may sound strange having beading only on one side of the bodice for a wedding gown; but trust me, clients will surprise you!

We know that it takes us 7 hours to bead the complete bodice front, logically speaking we would divide the bodice into 2 pattern units: left-front, and right-front. Using our example we would divide 7 hours by 2 to get the production time per pattern unit. It take us 3 ½ hours to bead each unit (left-front or right-front) which come to a total of $129.50 per unit in labor charges. To obtain the labor charge for the top quarter of the bodice is easy. Since it represents 25% of the front bodice unit, we multiply $129.50 by 25%.

What should you do if the design doesn't occupy the whole quarter panel? If it falls within the quarter panel, then it is charged as a quarter panel. This keeps pricing easy and manageable. Once you have the figure for the whole bodice pattern unit, you can make a chart for pricing interim segments of the bodice of the garment such as ¼ , ½ , ¾ and so on.

What about degrees of density? The number of beads will vary in terms of density from light, medium to heavy. Your chart will have three categories for density—light, medium and heavy. You will have to be the judge on how you determine degree of density. The point is you will have specific pricing for segments of a garment for lace, sequins and hand beading, etc. Our previous example represents a medium degree of density. Since we have 3 categories, labor charge for light would be half of what we charged for medium. If the clients gown required beading in the top quarter panel on both the right and left bodice, depending on the degree on density, you would simply multiply it times two.

Example: Heavy beading on top quarter panel of both the left and right bodice (center panel). On the chart go to the item entitled ¼ bodice pattern unit. Move your finger over to the heavy column; the price is $48.56 for one quarter panel. Since we are beading the left and right front panels, we need to multiply $48.56 by 2. The results would be: $48.56 x 2 = $97.12. The $97.12 figure becomes our labor charge for hand beading. You can make a similar chart for lace, sequins or anything requiring interim pricing.

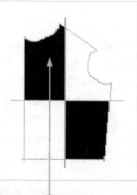

HAND BEADING			
ITEM	**DENSITY**		
	Light	**Medium**	**Heavy**
Single bodice pattern unit	64.75	129.50	194.25
¾ bodice pattern unit	48.56	97.13	145.69
½ bodice pattern unit	32.38	64.75	97.13
¼ bodice pattern unit	16.18	32.38	48.56
Have some fun—Make your own chart			

HAND BEADING

Heavy beading on top quarter panel of both the left and right bodice (center panel). The example shows right center quarter panel, you will also perform beading on the left quarter panel as well.

Using The Integrated Pricing Method

The time and motion study is complete, you have transferred all the values to the price list worksheet and multiplied them by your base labor rate; now it is time to make a formal price list. You would make categories and place your result under each. You will also have a section for miscellaneous items: zippers, hook and eye, etc. This becomes the tool by which you will charge the client for your labor.

A client has contracted with you to make a simple basic dress and train with a beaded bodice, pearl button back closure (18), and lace appliqué on the train, sleeves, neck and skirt. From your price list you would find the base labor charge for a basic dress, and add on for labor intensive design details. See the chart on the opposite page for details.

Using The Integrated Pricing Method

The chart below reflects labor charges for a simple basic dress and train with a beaded bodice, pearl button back closure (18), and lace appliqué on the train, sleeves, neck and skirt.

Labor charges from price list	
Item	**Labor Charge**
Dress	$ 375.00
Train	202.00
Pearl Buttons	75.00
Beading - Bodice	259.00
Lace – sleeves	145.00
Lace – neck	137.00
Lace – skirt	250.00
Lace – train	297.00
Total Labor	$ 1,740.00

Sewing for the bride has so many possibilities in terms of labor charges. It is one of the most complex fields in which pricing becomes a challenge for most professionals. The more creative a project, the more difficult it is to determine actual labor. Therefore, in some instances you will want to use the hourly method. However, you must still have some concept of your production time, thus giving you the ability to quote the client a reasonable estimate on fashion forward silhouettes.

Prior to embracing any one method, spend some time understanding how and why consumers make buying decisions. This was covered in the chapter entitled, *"Factors That Influence Consumer Spending."*

Be sure to test your method over a significant period of time. Make note of all the results, both from the consumer factor and the proprietary factor (see chapter one). Make any adjustments that will enhance your bottom line—your profit. Remember that pricing is not predicated upon mathematical formulas alone. Understanding all facets of pricing is a must.

Sewing For Children

Developing a pricing strategy when sewing for children is no different from one developed for custom sewing. The major element to be considered is your customer. What will make your business succeed is knowing what items you will produce and who you will produce them for. If you are sewing for children, and the child is very young, chances are the sole buying decision rests with the parents or grandparents. Essentially, you are sewing to please them. Your marketing campaign must take into consideration their buying habits. See *Marge's Unique Marketing Strategy* in this chapter.

As a business consultant, I worked with a client who sewed for children. She hired me because she didn't know how to price for profit. We reviewed her product offerings to determine who would be interested in her items. Her items were special she had designed a pinafore pattern, which she sold in conjunction with a basic little girl's dress. She only sewed for little girls, which I felt was too narrow a market with such a specialized item. We had our work cut out for us: First, to find the type of customers that would be repeat customers. Then, to effectively market to them. The following is an example from a previous section in this book. However, I thought it appropriate to repeat it and save you flipping back and forth. Please review Marge M. We shall examine how Marge solved her pricing and marketing problems.

Marge M's Big Mistake

December 10th at exactly 4 PM, Marge turned off her sewing machine, sat in her chair, looked around the room and burst into tears. Marge had been up all night working on a project. She was literally exhausted and saw very little progress. She had been in business for six months and had an inordinate number of clients--a situation most sewing professionals would kill for.

The customer had an appointment with Marge the next day to pick up her project, and Marge had at least three quarters left to complete—with no help in sight. The project itself was not that difficult, however, Marge's pricing method left no room for the intense labor design details requested by the customer. Her pricing policy was predicated upon the flat fee method. Marge had been making these items in mass and selling them to customers at a set price. When she started her business she didn't take into account that some customers would desire to incorporate their own personal style. Consequently, in doing so it would require extra time for labor intensive design details, and Marge's flat fee method didn't allocate for this. Needless to say, Marge had no frame of reference as to her actual production time, and therefore underestimated the time it would take her to complete the project. Let's examine the elements of Marge's problem.

Standard Item: *Her standard retail item consisted of a simple little girl's pinafore that took her no more than two hours to produce. The appeal for this item was in the way that she merchandised it over dresses through the use of vibrant colors and soft pastels. She would show the versatility gained in putting a pinafore over a little girls dress thus creating an entirely different look. She used color as a strong enticement. Occasionally she would add simple embellishments, however, nothing to the extent of what her customer ordered.*

Customer: *Ms. Wallingford, an affluent executive at Transcontinental Bank, had three granddaughters ranging from three to five years old. She had seen Marge's pinafores at a birthday party one of her customers had given. Her customer's daughter, Heather—six years old, was wearing one of Marge's standard pinafores in a pretty emerald green over a soft-pastel gingham dress. Being impressed with Marge's pinafores and eye for color, Ms. Wallingford booked an appointment with Marge.*

Customer's Order: *Three pinafores and three dresses, one for each granddaughter. The bodice would be smocked with contrasting thread to match the pinafore. Instead of a simple hem, she wanted a delicate lace trim. The dresses were simple and required nothing out of the ordinary. It was Marge's basic dress pattern that she used for all her retail orders.*

Labor Charges: *Marge charged her standard flat fee for the dresses, which was sufficient. She charged her standard flat fee for three of the pinafores.*

Problem: *It takes Marge two hours of production time to make each standard pinafore (no embellishments). Each pinafore with smocking and lace required an additional hour and a half, bringing the labor intensive design details to 4 ½ extra hours. Her flat fee method did not allow for the added production time, nor did she consider that fact when giving her client a completion time. Marge did not meet deadline, and had to call several customers to reschedule pick up times. Marge lost one of her very best customers in the process—Mrs. Cunningham. Marge wasn't aware that Mrs. Cunningham needed her daughter's pinafore to wear to a wedding.*

Marge's Loss: *First and foremost, she lost the integrity of her word; a valued customer, not to mention the financial loss suffered for inappropriate pricing. She endured stress from trying to meet an impossible deadline, and had to suffer feelings of helplessness.*

Project	Production Time	Labor Charge	3 Pinafores
Standard Pinafore: Flat Fee	*2.0 hours*	*$35.00*	*$105.00*
Smocking + Lace Trim	*1.5 hours*	*26.25*	*$78.75*
Standard + Smocking + Lace Trim	*3.5 hours*	*$61.25*	*$183.75*

Financial Loss			
Customer's Order	**Actual Production Cost**	**Billed Customer**	**Total Monetary Loss**
3 Pinafores/Smocking/Lace Trim	*$61.25 x 3 = $183.75*	*$35.00 x 3 = $105.00*	*$183.75 - $105.00 = $78.75*

Using the flat fee method, Marge only charged for the standard pinafore. Thus, creating a loss of $78.75 in total profit because her flat fee method did not allow for the labor intensive design details of smocking and lace trim.

Production Loss		
Actual Production Time	**Billed Hours**	**Total Hourly Loss**
3.5 hours x 3 = 10.5 hours	*2.0 hours x 3 = 6.0 hours*	*10.5 – 6.0 = 4.5 hours*

Marge lost 4.5 hours in total production caused by the extra labor intensive design details of smocking and lace trim. This loss could have yielded her 2 1/4 pinafores at the standard pinafore production time of $78.75 profit.

Note: See Marge's revised "Custom Sewing Price List

Marge's New Pricing Policy

Marge had a good number of first-time customers, however as is demonstrated from the example, she had problems with her pricing policy. We set out to revamp her pricing policy and construct a profit making price list. I had her to list her goals. Did she want to mass produce items and sell them retail or did she want to make custom items for clients, or do both. She decided to combine her efforts by selling retail and working exclusively with clients.

We took each market segment and made a price list. First we looked at her retail sales, which is how she got started. She made her basic dress in cotton pastel prints and gingham fabrics, and designed her famous pinafores in brilliant colors as an accent. We established a base labor rate using the pricing formula (see the chapter on Pricing Methods 101). Next we determined her production time on the basic dress and standard pinafore. Then we added all direct costs for fabric, lace, etc. Finally, we combined the direct cost with the labor charge and used the keystone method. The keystone method is used in retail pricing. It is where you mark up an item by a percentage to get the retail price. In true retail they keystone plus, meaning they add an additional fee to cover any extra costs. Example: fees for credit cards orders, gift wrapping, layaway, etc.

Pricing For Retail Items

The following is the formula used to obtain the retail price. Use the *Pricing Sheet** from *the Complete Set Of Forms* or the *Forms On Computer Disk* if you have it.

* These forms can be found in the Complete Set Of Forms or Forms on Computer Disk, see the order form at the end of this book.

1. Base Labor Rate x Production Time = Labor Charge
2. Labor Charge + Direct Cost = Net Cost
3. Net Cost x Markup Percentage (%) = Profit
4. Profit + Net Cost = Retail Price

Basic Dress:
      Base labor rate: $12   Production time: 2.5 hrs.   Direct cost: $5.00   Markup: 70%

Standard Pinafore:
      Base labor rate: $12   Production time: 2.0 hrs.   Direct cost: $3.00   Markup: 70%

Miscellaneous Design Details:
      Smocking: Base labor rate: $12   Production time: 1 hrs   Direct cost: $1.00
      Lace Trim: Base labor rate: $12   Production time: .5 hrs   Direct cost: $3.75

Marge's New Retail and Custom Price List

Marge's Retail Price List

Project (base labor rate $12)	Production Time	Labor Charge	Direct Cost	Net Cost	Mark Up 70%	Retail Price
Basic Dress	2.5 hrs	$30.00	$5.00	$35.00	$24.50	$59.50
Standard Pinafore	2.0 hrs	$24.00	$3.00	$27.00	$18.90	$45.90
Std Pinafore / Smocking / Lace	3.5 hrs	$42.00	$4.75	$46.75	$32.73	$79.48
Smocking	1.0 hrs	$12.00	$1.00	$13.00	N/A	N/A
Lace Trim	.5 hrs	$6.00	$3.75	$9.75	N/A	N/A

Marge's Unique Marketing Strategy

When Marge hired me, I explained to her that we had to come up with a unique approach to her business since she had such a narrow market. I devised several marketing strategies using personalized items and special products to give Marge's business a competitive edge. Her concept with the pinafores was excellent, however we still needed to give Marge's business something new and innovative. I had a number of ideas I wanted to share with Marge: Adding a decorative purse, gift wrapping services, custom greeting cards, personal embroidery, catalog, etc. Marge was open to my new ideas, working with her was a lot of fun.

You don't see a lot of little girls in pinafores these days. The baby-boomer generation, as well as their parents, wore them religiously. Knowing that we wanted to capitalize on a nostalgic craze, I had Marge target the mothers and grandmothers of that generation. The gingham and pastel printed dresses, accented by one of Marge's special jewel-tone pinafores where a big hit. She kept her retail items to a select assortment in various sizes. Thus making it easy for her to mass produce them. She purchased fabric in bulk, keeping excellent records of manufacturers inventories.

She hired an illustrator to mimic Norman Rockwell drawings for her new catalog, giving a vintage feel to the ads. She scanned in the drawing and printed the catalog on her color printer. She put a small graphic of the catalog cover on her envelope and stationery—exposure is the key.

Making the maximum use of her color printer and desktop publishing software, she offered beautiful custom greeting cards. To further specialize her business, she offered attractive gift wrapping services and garment bags. Marge had gone to a gift show and was able to negotiate with a sales rep to offer her a discount on specialized garment bags, boxes and wrapping paper. She purchased large quantities of paper and envelopes for her greeting cards from a wholesale paper company in her neighborhood. She went to her local office supply store and bought clear adhesive invoice pouches. She applied the pouches to the garment bags and put the personalized greeting cards inside. She also offered little girl's purses that fit on the belts of dresses for safety. Embroidery was a big hit, parents and grandparents always wanted their child's name embroidered either on the purse or the bodice of the pinafore.

Marge's retail and custom business enjoyed enormous success. She had to start subcontracting out retail and custom work. She sent her catalog to a commercial printer to keep pace with the demand. Her garment bags now have her custom logo complete with pouch attached. She has made templates of greeting cards and has them printed so all she has to do is customize the inside message. She has one person who now handles all personalized embroidery projects and makes the belts as well. Marge has a student come in part time for gift wrapping, and she even has the tissue paper that she uses for gift wrapping sporting her company name and logo. Way to go Marge!

What made Marge's business a success?

☐ Capitalizing on a theme
☐ Gift wrapping
☐ Special accessories (purse)
☐ Custom embroidered names
☐ Custom greeting cards
☐ Garment bags
☐ Jewel toned pinafores
☐ Dresses in soft pastel fabrics
☐ Knowing her customer
☐ Correct pricing for retail and custom clients

Marge's Custom Sewing Price List

Labor Charge	Production Time	Labor Charge	Labor Charge	Production Time	Labor Charge
Basic Dress - Gathered Skirt	2.5 hrs	$30.00	Standard Pinafore	2.0 hrs	$24.00
Basic Dress – Pleated	3.5 hrs	$42.00	Std Pinafore / Smocking / Lace	3.5 hrs	$42.00
Long Sleeves	.5 hrs	$6.00	Smocking	1.0 hrs	$12.00
Embellished Collar	.5 hrs	$6.00	Lace Trim	.5 hrs	$6.00
Ruffled trim – Skirt	1.5 hrs	$18.00	Multicolor/ Special Fabrics	.5 hrs	$6.00
Petticoat	1.0 hrs	$12.00	Plaids	1.0 hrs	$12.00
Petticoat – Lace Trim	1.5 hrs	$18.00	Stripes	1.0 hrs	$12.00
Bodice – Lace Inset	.5 hrs	$6.00	Bodice Lining	.5 hrs	$6.00
Lace Inset – Skirt	1.0 hrs	$12.00	Skirt Lining	.5 hrs	$6.00
Sash	.5 hrs	$6.00	Buttons	each	*$0.50
Belt	.5 hrs	$6.00	Hook / eye set	each	*$0.50
Belted Purse	1.5 hrs	$18.00	Snap set	each	*$0.50
Custom Greeting Card	Per Card	*$3.75	Zipper	each	*$4.90
Consultation	Per Hour	*$12.00	Embroidered Name	each	*$5.00
Gift Wrap	Per Box	*$3.00	Garment Bag	each	*$3.00

* Means per unit of measure (hour, box, each, etc.)

The bottom line: To sew for children you need to provide something fresh and different to give the consumer a reason to do business with you. Find a niche as Marge did and capitalize on it. Market with the ultimate consumer in mind. Ask yourself: "What would inspire them to do business with me?" Refer to the chart on "Factors Influencing Consumer Spending," in this book. Be innovative as Marge was in offering gift wrapping, custom cards, embroidered names, etc. These are personalized touches that consumers are looking for.

Is There A Profit In A Personal Pattern Line?

Part One

What You Need To Know To get Started

Elegant, Classic Clothing With a Contemporary Twist

Clothing Designs by *La Fred*

Fred Bloebaum, short for La Fred, launched the release of her patterns line, *"Clothing Designs by La Fred."* Her patterns provide elegant, and classic clothing that have contemporary lines and are easy to construct. Fred is a regular instructor at *The Sewing Workshop* in San Francisco. Fred is also a contributor to *Threads* magazine. Her specialties include tailoring; sewing with specialty fabrics; figure analysis and wardrobe selection; and interpreting fine designer sewing techniques.. Fred is also a member of The Professional Association of Custom Clothiers. We asked Fred if there is really a profit in having a personal pattern line, and here is what she had to say:

What motivated you to start your own pattern line? I had been teaching sewing for five to six years and loved it, but felt it wasn't bringing in the amount of money I would like and thought I needed a product as well. I also hadn't seen a pattern with my style and I felt there was a niche for my pattern.

What steps did you take to launch your business? I mainly used trial and error. I had no set plan in mind. Networking helped the most. I started with one pattern and when I got it designed I met someone who could do the grading and from there I was introduced to others who could help. It grew from talking to people and I developed a team from there.

What are the expenses associated with starting your own pattern line? There are your basic up front costs associated with starting any business such as, publicity, mail box rental, professional publicity photos and other business costs. The costs particular to having a pattern line are paying a grader, illustrators for the technical drawings, graphic designs editing, testers who wear the pattern and sew it for ease, cover design and illustrations, printing and production costs, advertising, research and development. Before a pattern is released, I have sewn it five or six times, and this is where the majority of my costs come in. I am a very small business; I pay all the people that provide services for my pattern line, which allows me to maintain all of the profit.

What suggestions do you have for getting started? First, begin by fine tuning your patterns by trying them out and showing them to others. Get people excited about your products. The most important part is testing, testing and more testing. Be sure to test at the extremes of size as well as in the middle of the size range. Work it out from there and decide how much you're willing to do yourself and how much you want to outsource to others.

What are the pros and cons of pattern design?

   Cons: You must have a lot of startup capital to begin with. The more money you have up front in making the patterns look professional will pay off in the end. I was unable to qualify for an SBA loan in the beginning, so I had to find the funding other places. The other problem I have noticed is that the sales seem to be cyclical so some times of the year I sell less. I have to budget to have money to carry over for these slow times.

   Pros: I feel good about the response from people who have made the patterns. I fill the sewing needs of people in various size ranges. My patterns provide comfort and the ability to look good on many people. Another benefit is that the money is great! It has enabled me to have a profitable business. I never had a profitable year when I was simply teaching sewing, but now that I have begun selling patterns as well as teaching, I have been making a profit!

What is your pricing formula for your patterns? It's really hit or miss because I have to determine the price of the pattern prior to having it printed so it can be printed on the pattern itself. Sometimes, I have to guess how much to charge. I have a basic formula I try to follow by figuring the up front costs as being half of the wholesale price. I figure out how many pieces I will need to print and whether they are lined as well as the number of technical drawings in the instruction sheet; the more I have, the higher the price I must charge. One reason is because I have to pay more to have it printed. Also, if I have several versions for the pattern and I show them all on the cover, then it will cost more for illustrations. I also have a price range of ten to fifteen dollars in which I am most comfortable selling my patterns. I am not comfortable selling my patterns for more than fifteen dollars, because I feel my patterns are simple and I would price myself out of a certain part of my market.

What type of advertising, marketing and promotions do you employ? I originally advertised in several magazines and publications; I have narrowed it down to a few which I get a steady response. They are *Sew News* and *Threads*. They are two of the most expensive places to advertise, but I get a fair and steady response. I also put a brochure in every order. I am often asked to donate patterns to different sewing events and will send brochures along to be given out. I sell at industry consumer shows and I have brochures at my booth to give away as well. The best source has been having my patterns reviewed in *Sew News*, *Threads* and *Creative Machine*. I have had reviews on my pattern line and got good responses from them.

How do you handle the distribution of your patterns? I do direct mail and I have some wholesale accounts. I don't sell to chains. I am not interested in being sold through a distributor, I feel I will lose control of the way my product is marketed. I began by contacting all the fabric stores I knew of and told them of the availability of my patterns. Some of my wholesale orders came through word-of-mouth, reviews and ads. Wholesale accounts pay half of the retail cost with a minimum order of six patterns, and I charge for shipping as well.

Who prints your patterns? McCall's Pattern Company prints my patterns. I had known others who used them and my graphic artists and my grader knew how to get in contact with them. I had to fill out a credit form, but that was all. I pay them to print the patterns, so they have no say over what I do because I am not part of McCall's; just a customer. They have really been great and accommodating to work with. When I've run into problems paying the total amount up front, they have understood and worked with me.

Can you give resources for other individuals to start their own pattern line? I am always happy to share the names of my people. I have provided my contacts at the end of this chapter. The best way to find people to work with is through the sewing industry associations. For instance, I am a member of PACC and this is where I found my pattern grader and from there she had resources for others in the pattern design field. I recommend going to your local guild or PACC to find people to work with. Another good resource is through community colleges that teach fashion design where you can take classes to improve your skills as well as putting you in contact with others who can help.

Is there anything else you would like to say to inform or suggest to others? If you have a vision, and you are really interested in having your own personal pattern line—it is a good time to do it! People are very into small pattern companies right now and it is a good time to pursue it— keep your vision. Be aware, and know that what you do is unique, and know how to position yourself and your product. The more time and effort you put in at the front end, the better it will pay off in the long run.

La Fred

Fred Bloebaum's Resources

Graphic Designer: Lozano Printing 408-995-5906	Lynda Lozano 365 Willow #1 San Jose, CA 95110
Pattern Grading - Computerized Patternwork: Laughing Moon Mercantile 408-223-0593	JoAnn Bowser 2991 Densmore Dr. San Jose, CA 95148
Fashion Illustrator: Kathleen McCarney 925-820-4563	305 Adagio Dr Danville, CA 94526
Editor and Pattern Tester: A Great Notion Communications 408-265-7074	Cheryle Custer 5720 Hark Manor Dr. San Jose, CA 95118
Pattern Printer: McCall's Pattern Company 785-776-4041	615 McCall Rd. Manhattan, KS 66502

La Fred's Patterns
Call 800-795-8999 or 510-893-6811

Part Two

Pattern Printing

Fred inspires you to want to go out and start your very own pattern line. The good news is that if done correctly you can earn a profit and share your gift of designing with others. Keep in mind that all costs associated with launching your venture must be factored into your pricing. Let's take a look at some examples of the cost involved in printing the pattern.

McCall's Commercial Printing Department

The McCall's Pattern Company has a commercial printing department where they specialize in printing patterns for entrepreneurs. During my interview with them they shared a wealth of helpful information for getting a pattern printed with their company.

1. What is the first step in getting your pattern printed by McCall's?
2. How much time does it take?
3. What affects the prices?

What is the first step in getting your pattern printed by McCall's? You should order McCall's kit which outlines all the steps and requirements for getting started, complete with an overview of the process. However, it doesn't list prices; you will have to contact them directly for exact quotes. You can send your designs to them on disk format. Consult with them on the types of formats required. You should also know what type of tissue paper you want to use as well (8 lb. Brown, 8 ½ lb. Bleach White, etc.)

How much time does it take? It generally takes around three weeks to complete, however a lot depends on how well organized and complete your packages are. If you follow their requirements, you should see a completed pattern in the three week time span.

What affects the prices? As with anything you purchase, there are variables. It should be reiterated that for exact pricing you will need to speak directly with McCall's on a case-by-case basis. However, for the purpose of illustration, I will give you some factors that may affect pricing. Paper prices go up and down from year to year. Also, if you need to see more than one proof of a pattern, or if you find that you have made an error and need to change something after film or plates have been made, the price can also go up. The total quantity that you are printing can affect the price, and the price quoted does not include freight charges which vary according to weight, distance shipped and how the patterns may be shipped.

What is included when you have your pattern printed?
1. One four-color printed pattern envelope (front and back)
2. One instruction sheet
3. One printed pattern tissue
4. Each additional printed pattern tissue is extra

Contact information for McCall's Commercial Division
McCall's Pattern Company
615 McCall's Rd.
Manhattan, KS 66502
785-776-4041

Jane Ambrose's—Pattern Printing Strategy

Jane Ambrose recently launched her own pattern line—Warm Heart Patterns, featuring children's coordinated clothing. Jane shares how she went about getting her patterns printed.

There are a number of ways to go—depending on what kind of capital you want to spend. I have talked to several small pattern companies who have gone to Simplicity to have them print patterns and instructions. The only problem is they have minimums that are around 1000 units per size range. I think that is quite expensive if you are the new kid on the block. I'd prefer to make less per unit and not invest that kind of money for a thousand pieces that might not sell.

For my patterns, I had them done in 24 X 35 format and have been only getting photocopies of the originals. These are anywhere from $1.50 to $2.00 each which is far more than having them printed by either a printing company or a pattern company. There are two reasons I did mine that way: The best prices are based on printing 250 to 1000 units, and I really didn't know which patterns would be popular. I decided to test market first before spending the money. I purchased plastic bags and then inserted the folded pattern along with the instructions; and it's fairly easy to hire someone to do this for you.

Jane makes a valid point. Although you could get your patterns printed for under $1.50 by going to a commercial pattern printer, until you are sure how the market will respond, it is best to print small quantities and test market prior to investing large sums of money. However, considering patterns retail around $15 dollars, even at $2.00 per pattern cost, you still make a significant profit. To answer the question: Is there a profit in having a personal pattern line—I think the answer is a resounding "Yes!".

Below are samples of Jane's pattern line *Warm Heart* and her books. She also has business forms. To order or get a current listing of her full line of patterns and forms, please call 1-800-795-8999. See order form at the end of this book.

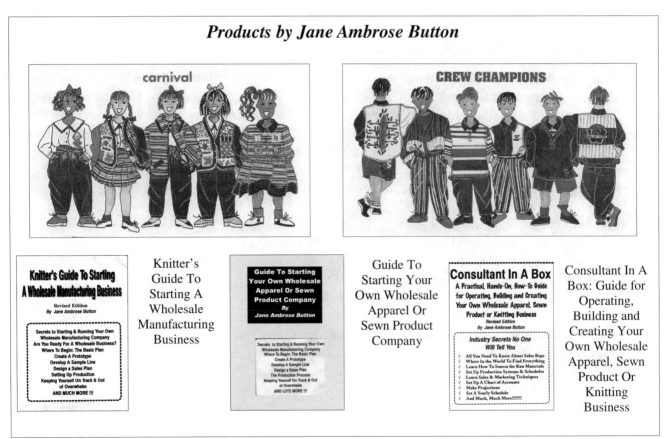

Products by Jane Ambrose Button

Pricing For Consignment and Retail

Jane Ambrose is multi-talented; she is a business consultant specializing in creative product development, production, merchandising, pricing, costing, sales and marketing. She started Warm Heart, a wholesale apparel business, which grew into a national brand name. She recently launched her own pattern line—Warm Heart Patterns, featuring children's coordinated clothing. In the previous chapter, Jane shared her strategy for launching her personal pattern line.

Sewing professionals have yearned for information to help them effectively price their items for the wholesale market. In this chapter, Jane shares her expertise regarding pricing items for consignment and retail.

Pricing—Consignment and Retail

Companies that manufacture small quantities of sewn or knitted products inevitably come up with the issue of pricing their products. Generally, the scenario is similar, no matter what the product. A manufacturer (you) with a well made, professional-looking product, popular with a small audience, decides to expand the circle by going to the next level selling wholesale, on consignment, opening a retail store or even starting a web page (a cyber store). The question I often hear from small companies in my consulting business is: How do I know my prices are correct? How do I price the products so I make a profit *and* am competitive enough so the goods will sell *and* the consumer considers the product a value for the price? Some of these manufacturers have only produced the goods themselves and are quite unfamiliar with the process of selling their products on a wholesale level.

The price you set for you product must be one where you make a decent profit and the store to whom you sell or consign your goods to can also make a decent profit. You must both win. Remember that a store will at least double the wholesale price (a term called keystone) to come up with a retail price and a store who accepts consignment will generally take anywhere from 40% to 60% of the retail price. Always keep this information in mind when formulating your price. When you think wholesale, remember that you are selling at this price to the store who will charge a retail price. When you sell on consignment; you decide the retail price and the store gets a percentage of that price. For purposes of discussion, the majority of the information here refers to "wholesale price" because once you determine your wholesale price you can, in fact, easily determine the retail price for consignment because what you want to end up with is the wholesale amount in your pocket. The thing to remember when pricing wholesale for the retail market is someone else is going to make money from your product, unless of course you sell your own product at retail.

Pricing has such an impact on sales—either negatively or positively. It is important to know how to come up with a wholesale price from the very beginning. When I first started my company I knew little about pricing except for some advice by a lady named "Betty" who also had her own business. She told me, "never charge less than three times what it costs to make something" and "always start at top dollar because it's nearly impossible to raise prices, and people are suspicious when you lower prices." I still think of her advice when I price, but there is much more to it than these simple statements. Incidentally, Betty manufactured a beautiful line of Christmas stockings and made a small fortune.

There are no simple answers or magic formulas. Pricing is ultimately a subjective issue. The "right price" is whatever someone is willing to pay. But, is that "right price" also going to make you a profit, and will it be one that you can live with? Pricing for the wholesale market requires an understanding of three elements: cost of goods sold, your target market, and your competition. It's a chicken and egg situation, you need to price so that consumers will buy the item, but you also need to make a profit. In order to establish a price, you must know how much you are spending to manufacture it, if your product is needed in the market, and what your competition is doing with a similar product. All three of these issues are critical to setting your price.

Keys to Determining Price Points for the Wholesale Market:

- ❖ **Start with your product and Identify Your Target Market** *Is your product something this market will want to buy ?*

- ❖ **Identify your competition** *What are the price points of similar items and at what price are they selling the best?*

- ❖ **Determine your Cost of Goods Sold** *How much are you really paying to manufacture?*

How to Know Your Target Market—Who wants your product anyway?

Start by knowing your target market. Just who is your customer and how does she/he decide to make purchases? In general, the public spends money on a product because of their emotional reaction to the product. In other words, they purchase an item based on how they think it is going to make them feel. Once they feel they must have whatever it is, then they justify the price. Attempt to identify what will move your ultimate customer to purchase your product. Take a look at the habits and desires of that market and direct the design of your product to the consumer.

This part of your pricing may not seem very important to you. You may take your product for granted. After all, your friends like it and some of them have paid good money for it. Please don't just assume that the rest of the world wants to pay money for your product. Examine and evaluate your product to be sure that your selected target market wants to buy it. A mistake I see small companies make is that they try to make an existing product fit into a market rather than filling a need for a particular market.

There's a whole mentality and psychology of spending that you simply cannot ignore. Chances are, if you are making a sewn product in a small business, it is not your idea to compete against price points with Target, or Wal-Mart, but rather to make a very special product for a certain upscale customer. Unless you have bottomless resources to come up with a mass market product, your best plan is to select a niche market and sell to that market.

I did, however, once work with a company that did have resources to do just that. Dolls have become extremely popular in the last several years. There are collectors, doll classes, magazines about dolls—dolls everywhere. Some friends of mine who actually owned a furniture making company saw an opening in the market. They saw that there was potentially a huge market for porcelain dolls at a popular price. There had been very expensive ones in the market and they figured that it was time that well-made dolls at a popular price would be a hit. They researched the market extensively and found that the customers who shopped at certain stores such as Fred Meyer, K-Mart and Costco, would buy dolls that retailed for under $20. They were able to find production offshore, meet specifications of buyers for these large stores and have been manufacturing beautiful porcelain dolls for several years and selling them to large mass market merchants. They now make an 18" doll of vinyl also at a popular price. The point is they found a need in the market and then filled it. They know their buyer wants a good quality item at an affordable price.

Please don't think, "Well, my customer shops at boutiques and better stores so these are the target markets," look beyond the store front itself. What you need to understand here is who is going to buy your product and what are their emotional reasons for purchasing your product. Just who is your mythical customer and where does he or she spend money? Where do you think this person shops, list some of the places in your area. Just what motivates this person to make a purchase? What kind of emotional attachment are they linking with your product? Perhaps it screams nostalgia or there's something about it that appeals to the buyer on an emotional level. If it appeals to them on an emotional level then is the price something they would think about before making the purchase?

People buy products because they have some value for them. They buy on emotion and justify on logic. What is the value of your product and how would your customer justify purchasing it?

A client I worked with had a small company with a unique design for a terry cloth bib. The competition in the bib market is fierce because it's a gift item sold in department stores and mass market outlets as well as boutiques. A bib is often a point-of-sale item, meaning it's near the cash register and as a customer is purchasing other goods they happen on the cute bib and buy it impulsively.

Even though the design was unique, the sales for this little company were just not where they wanted them to be. We examined the gift market for babies and then specifically narrowed it down to University stores where they sell products with University or College logos. The company ended up getting a license agreement with a large University to produce bibs with the University's logos and slogans. Price was no object to the alumni who supported their teams by buying products for their children and grandchildren. The bib company went on to get license agreements from other schools and eventually made other products catering to the same market. They built their business around a certain niche and catered specifically to their needs. They redefined their target market, then redesigned their product (by adding the logo) and ultimately were able to restructure their prices to make a good profit.

> **"QUIZ"**
> Regarding commission, a store who accepts consignment will generally
> take anywhere from 40% to _____ percentage of the retail price?

Identify your competition — conduct a Market Analysis

You'll want to begin by determining the retail prices of products similar to the one you're making. Compare your product to similar ones in the marketplace. Your particular design or idea might be innovative, creative and seem brand new, but very likely there is something out there that is of a similar nature, at least for comparison. Your market analysis is much like what a real estate agent would do in pricing your home for sale. The agent would compare recent sales and listings of similar houses in your geographic area based on a number of different criteria, i.e. square footage, number of bedrooms, bathrooms, etc. This is what you are about to do, only with products.

Let's say you make beautiful children's smocked dresses. You've been making these for your child and for many of your friends' children. Everyone thinks your designs are unique and you finally decide you'd like to take the plunge and wholesale them to some of the children's shops in the area. Make a list of the stores in your geographic area that carry children's dresses. These stores could be specialty children's boutiques, gift stores or upscale department stores. Take some time to research these stores for dresses in your category. And by the way, while you're at it check these stores out as your potential customers.

> **"ANSWER"**
> Consignment will generally take anywhere from
> 40% to 60% percentage of the retail price.

Become a detective and take notes of the following:

- ◆ **Check out the retail prices** based on sizes so you know the retail prices of the size ranges you are anticipating you will manufacture. *Note that in clothing size ranges can make a difference in price because of the materials usage, so be sure you compare apples to apples. That goes as well for anything where material usage would be affected.*

- ◆ **Consider the quality of the materials** that are used. What is the fabric content? Quality 100% Pima (expensive and soft) cotton, or is it a poly/cotton blend, linen, silk or something else. How does this compare to your product?

- ◆ **What are the complexities of the designs**? Is the smocking better or more complex than yours or is it less intricate? Is the smocking done by hand or is it machine made, or can you tell?

- ◆ **How is the general quality** of the item?

- ◆ **Are there any special features or touches.** These might be a special hang tag that tells about the person who made it; maybe a hair bow that comes with the dress or a small embroidery on the collar. Is there something that adds a little special touch? What about your dress, do you have any special touches that add value?

- ◆ **Look at the tags inside.** Where is the garment manufactured? What are the care instructions (does it need to be dry cleaned?) and content of the fabric.

- ◆ **Ask a salesperson questions (if you can discreetly).** You might want to know if they've carried a brand for a while, how well these dresses sell and the like. Sometimes you can get a lot of information from a salesperson about a product.

This last element is one of the most important because regardless of how much the list price is, you'll need to know the price at which the product sells the best:

- ◆ **Check Sales Racks and Off-Price Stores.** What didn't sell? And once it goes on sale what is the sale price? You can almost learn more about price by looking at these racks at the end of the season than anywhere else. Additionally, there are numerous discount stores such as Loehmanns, Ross, and TJ Maxx. See what you find in these stores. Are there similar products and where are they priced? Typically, manufacturers sell goods that are left over at the end of the season to the discount stores, so this is a good way to see what items were not shipped. Now, the discount stores are savvy and they will only buy items they know are popular and can move quickly, so that should give you a good indication about what will sell at what price.

Even if you're only going to sell in your own geographic area, expand your search and look for similar items in catalogs (a great source), magazines and on the internet. Expand your search even more by looking at stores out of your area when you travel and ask your friends or relatives who live out of town to help you with your detective work. If there is a trade center near you or you visit a town where there is one, spend time researching wholesale products. Even better, attend a trade show where you can really sleuth out information from many sources all at once. See what buyers are buying and what prices are acceptable for your type of product.

Now you should have some valuable information together so you can make a **comparison** between what the market has available and your product. This comparison is where you may even decide to reevaluate your thinking. You may decide you need to upgrade your materials, you may decide not to make what you had thought about making because there are already too many, or someone else is already doing it better and cheaper than you possibly could. Perhaps you will decide to revise your entire product.

When my company, Warm Heart, began we started by manufacturing hand-loomed sweaters and hats made with acrylic (orlon) yarn. We started small and sales were good in the children's boutique stores. After about two years the same stores ordered fewer sweaters and through our investigation we found that the stores were buying the more expensive cotton sweaters instead of acrylic. You may not recall, but there was a time when mothers did not appreciate the virtues of natural fibers and especially cotton. The consumer mentality was that cotton shrinks, it's hard to take care of, etc. Fortunately, through consumer education the upscale buyer realized that 100% cotton was not so hard to clean, was better for baby's skin and for the environment. The market changed and so did we. We found a very soft cotton yarn that was washing machine friendly and changed our fabrication completely. An interesting thing happened here, we increased our prices, partially because our raw materials cost us more, but we were also able to increase our margins because the consumer was willing to pay a higher price for the perceived value in a 100% cotton sweater.

A tabletop company I worked with wanted to make table runners, napkins, placemats and table-cloths. Before actually going into business they did careful research on the prices, designs and materials of their competition. When they finally started their business they had a hit with the high-end stores because they carefully chose their designs and fabrics to be different than what was currently in the market. Even though their prices were much higher than other similar products, they were the only manufacturers who made tabletop items with these types of fabrics. They have stayed competitive with their pricing because they are consistently staying ahead of their competition. Consequently, they are viewed as a leader in their industry and are able to charge more.

My children's apparel company used to manufacture turtlenecks to go underneath our sweaters. All of our turtlenecks had embroidery or a screen print which matched the sweater. As a consequence, many of our customers purchased both the sweater and the matching turtleneck. We did however, have requests for solid color turtlenecks from several customers. They wanted the colors to match up with our sweaters and they also wanted to mix and match the turtlenecks and be sure they were delivered at the same time as our sweaters (rather than buying them from another vendor). We failed to do our research on solid color turtlenecks. If we had we would have found that we could not make solid color turtlenecks at an acceptable price and make a profit margin within acceptable limits. Our turtlenecks with embroideries sold in spite of their higher price because they matched our unique sweater designs. We made the turtlenecks in solids but found we couldn't compete with GAP, J.C. Penney or any of the large markets even though the customers said they wanted them from us. We ended up selling them off at huge discounts to discount stores and lost money. We learned a very valuable lesson in pricing from this experience.

Cost of Goods Sold — Number Crunching your component parts

The most critical element in determining profit is your **cost of goods sold**. These are all the component parts of your product including labor. Once you know your costs you will be able to calculate a multitude of information about your price and your product.

In conjunction with your cost of goods sold, you need to take into account the commission you will pay for consignment sales and the commission you will pay a sales rep should you decide to hire one. Once you know all of these component parts, you can be confident in setting a price and knowing exactly what your profit margins will be. Having done your planning and homework well, you can make decisions on whether or not to manufacture an item and know when you can make big profits. Having this knowledge under your belt is a powerful confidence builder in setting your final price structure.

How much are you spending to manufacture? How to figure your Total Cost of Goods Sold:

How often have you gone into a store and seen something for sale and you say to yourself, "Oh that's so expensive; I could make that for less!" Perhaps you could make it for less but when you analyze all of the component parts, including getting paid or paying someone else to do the labor, the question is: "Could you not only make it for that price but could you sell it and make a profit?" The two are not the same.

Before you can determine what you are going to charge someone for your goods, you need to know *exactly* how much you paid to make them. In my consulting business, I am always amazed when a client has no handle on the basics of costing out their goods. Somehow they mysteriously leave out certain key items like their own labor or packaging or they actually fudge on the cost of their fabric. It seems we all try to make ourselves look better but this is not the time to do that. When you add up your costs, be sure to be brutally honest with yourself and as they say in carpentry, "measure twice — cut once."

So, let's start from the beginning. Make a list of materials that you might need in order to manufacture your product. This is called a *Bill of Materials* and in the garment industry this itemization is used to determine a cost per unit. It is the same for other sewn products.

- Fabric — list all of them used in the product
- Thread: How much thread is used per piece (often in the industry the thread is included in the labor)
- Trims: yardage, snap tape, ribbon, seam binding, embroideries,
- Findings: buttons, snaps, zippers,
- Labels & Hangtags
- Packaging: Plastic bags, hangers,
- Labor: All labor for sewing, finishing and packaging

Though there is software that is specific to the garment industry that will track all of these things and more, it is quite costly and you are better off in the beginning as a small manufacturer learning how to do all of this by hand. The best way to go about this is to use a spreadsheet. Here is the information you will need to have:

Fabric Usage / Yardage: How many yards of fabric will you use per unit? If you are using more than one fabric, you will need to list each one separately. (i.e. fabric 1; fabric 2 etc.)

Fabric Cost per yard: What does each fabric cost per yard? Be sure to include the cost of shipping in this yardage if you paid $3.00 per yd. for the fabric and an additional $.10 per yd. to have it shipped to your facility, you have now paid $3.10 per yard.

Note: Shipping Costs are really hidden costs that add up. You might think 10 cents is not a lot of money but if you are manufacturing 300 units, that's $30 that would be unaccounted for in your pricing. It's easy to determine the cost of shipping per yard which is your unit of measurement. If you've ordered 100 yds of fabric and the shipping charges are $15 divide the shipping charges by the number of yards. In this case it would be $.15 per yard.

Total Fabric Cost: Multiply the fabric usage by the cost per yard to get your total fabric cost. If you have more than one fabric, multiply each one out and then add them all up together to get the total for fabric.

Trims Usage:	Same as for Fabric as listed above or by unit if the trims are embroideries, patches etc. So, if you are using lace by the yard treat it like a fabric as shown above and if you are purchasing rosettes count the number per piece.
Trims Cost per yard:	Same as above for Fabric with exception of per unit items
Total Trims:	Multiply the cost per unit by the number of units for each trim. Again, if using more than one trim be sure to add them all together.
Findings Usage:	You may have several of these. If you are making a garment you might have several snaps, buttons or a zipper.
Findings Cost per unit:	What is the cost per unit of each one.
Total Cost Findings:	Multiply total usage by cost per unit to figure total cost.
Hangtag:	Usually there is only one hangtag per garment or product, however you could have more than one. Be sure to identify the cost per unit and add it in even though it may be only a few cents.
Labels:	There are care labels, size tabs, washing instructions etc. Be sure to identify how many of each is used and then identify the cost of each.
Labor:	The cost you need to pay someone to manufacture your product per unit. This would include cutting, making and possibly packaging (plastic bags, hangers, etc.) your product.

COST OF GOODS SOLD
Take all of the above and add them together. Here's an example using a size 4 children's dress

Dress Size 4 Style #SP400					
	description	cost per yd/unit	ship per yd/unit	usage	total
Fabric 1	cotton print	$ 3.00	$ 0.10	2.00	$ 6.20
Fabric 2	cotton check	$ 2.65	$ 0.05	0.45	$ 1.22
Fabric 3	Interfacing	$ 1.50	$ 0.05	0.15	$ 0.23
Trim 1	1" lace	$ 1.25	$ 0.02	4.00	$ 5.08
Trim 2	1/2" lace	$ 0.99	$ 0.02	2.00	$ 2.02
Buttons	size 24 Line	$ 0.04	$ 0.005	6	$ 0.28
Hang tag 1	product info	$ 0.10	$ 0.001	1	$ 0.10
Label 1	size tab	$ 0.03	$ 0.001	1	$ 0.03
Label 2	company label	$ 0.15	$ 0.001	1	$ 0.15
Label 2	care label	$ 0.05	$ 0.001	1	$ 0.05
Labor	Cutting & Making	$ 6.00	$ -	1	$ 6.00
Packaging	hanger	$ 0.05	$ 0.010	1	$ 0.06
Packaging	plastic bag	$ 0.005	$ 0.001	1	$ 0.01
Total COST OF GOODS					**$ 21.42**

HOW TO USE THIS INFORMATION

Now that you know your costs down to the penny you can use this information to help you determine your final prices. It is generally common practice in most manufacturing companies to use margins as a measurement instead of markup to figure your profit. If you are unfamiliar with the difference between the two, the following explanation should help.

The difference between **margin** and **markup** is what you use as the base measure. For example, if you have cost of $6.00 and sell for $10.00 you have profit of $4.00. **Margin** means, "what portion of my sales dollar is profit?" In this case, margin is 4 divided by 10 or 40%. **Markup** means "how much have I put on top of (marked up) my cost?" In this case markup equals 4 divided by 6 or 67%.

Using the margin method for the size 4 dress we can now price the dress according to industry standards or better. The garment industry standards, if you look them up, show the standards to be a 35% margin. This includes all kinds of manufacturers from mass merchants on up. My strong suggestion to you as a small manufacturer—likely catering to the specialty market - is to stay with a margin of 50% or better. I like 55% or better even more. So let's look at our example. The total cost of goods is $21.42. If we want to determine the price using a 35% margin we use a formula as follows: 100%-35%=65% so you divide the cost by 65% to reach a wholesale price of $32.95. Your profit in dollars and cents is $11.53 but your margin is 35%. Using a spread sheet with your formula built into your computer you can see what your wholesale price would be based on a variety or margins: *COGS = Cost of Goods Sold

Margin	CoGS	Wholesale	Keystone Retail (double)*
35%	21.42	$32.95	$65.90
40%	21.42	$35.70	$71.40
45%	21.42	$38.95	$77.90
50%	21.42	$42.84	$85.68
55%	21.42	$47.60	$95.20

Please note that this price would be the sales price for a consignment sale before the retail establishment takes their percentage.

Now here is where your market analysis or comparison shopping of your competition really comes into play. Look at what similar items retail for in your market. If dresses for this market retail the best at under $100 you might go for it and charge a wholesale price of $47.60 so the store can retail the dress for under $100. However if the retail price is usually $50 or less you are going to have to reevaluate your costs to see if you can lower them in some category. Some ways in which you can do this are:

- *Work with your labor prices by getting a better price from your contractor*
- *Change the design to make the dress less complicated*
- *Select a different fabric that's less expensive*
- *Select different trims than you're already using to cut the price*
- *Take off some of the trims all together*

If none of these ideas get the price down to where you can make acceptable margins, go back to square one and come up with another product. Absolutely do not put yourself in a position where you are not going to make a decent profit. No matter what anyone tells you, you can't make it up on volume. No matter how emotionally attached you are to the product, you are going to have to rethink your plan.

The Sales Rep Factor

Now one important element we have not yet discussed is the sales commission charged by the sales rep. This will greatly impact your total margin. When calculating your final wholesale price (not commission for consignment) you are going to need to factor in the cost of doing business with a rep selling your goods.

In the garment industry standard commissions are approximately 10% to 15% of the wholesale price. Reps will also often try to charge more than this by asking for a "show room fee" which is a monthly fee they charge you to have your goods in their showroom. The gift and accessory industry works on a 15% to 20% commission. The commission is a percentage taken off the wholesale price. For example if you are selling the sampled dress to a store for $47.60 and your commission is 10%, then the sales rep would receive $4.76 for each dress sold to the store. As you can see, this is a large chunk of your profits, so you had better account for this in your pricing.

There are two ways you can do this. The first is to make sure your margins are at least 50%. The second way is to actually account for the sales commission in the price point. So, your formula would then include the commission. You would calculate your wholesale price with your margins as above and then divide by 100% minus 10% (whatever the commission rate would be) which in this case is 90% or .9.

From the example of the dress above the price changes when you factor in the 10% commission:

Margin	COGS	Wholesale	Wholesale	(REP) Retail
35%	21.42	$32.95	$36.61	$ 73.22
40%	21.42	$35.70	$39.67	$ 79.34
45%	21.42	$38.95	$43.28	$ 86.56
50%	21.42	$42.84	$47.60	$ 95.20
55%	21.42	$47.60	$52.89	$105.78

Now that dress that needed to retail for under $100 will still wholesale at $47.60 but your total margin will be 50% instead of 55%. You have factored in your commission, and that is now included in your pricing structure. On the other hand, now if your retail price needed to be $50 or less you are totally out of the ball game and it will take a lot of changes to get your costs down to fall within these parameters.

SELLING YOUR PRODUCT

You will always have choices to make on how to set your final wholesale prices, which impacts the retail price the store charges or what you set as a price on a consignment sale before commission. Now that you know where your price points should be in order for you to make a profit, you need to make some educated decisions on how to sell your product.

I once taught a seminar where a lady asked me the question: "How do I get someone to sell my product because all I want to do is make it?" My answer to her was in short; either get a partner or work for someone else. What she wanted to do was to keep busy by doing what she liked to do — not have a business. When you are running your own small business you must know how to do everything, or at the very least understand it. One of these items is selling.

In the beginning I always suggest that the owner of the small company go out and sell their product themselves. By doing this, you will learn a great deal about your customers, your product and what the market is up to. You can't learn these things by sitting in your factory, you have to be proactive. Whether you are selling wholesale to a retail establishment or putting your goods on consignment in a store, you are still selling.

Even if you do begin by selling your own products, eventually you need to put a plan together on how to sell your product. Do you want to hire a sales rep? If you do, what should you know about reps? Should you sell on Consignment and how does this work? Just what do these choices entail and are there alternatives? Selling has changed over the last several years for a variety of reasons and if you are entering the retail market you must know how this could affect you and your small business.

We now have a very savvy consumer. The public is not stupid at all. They understand quality, know what things cost, they research prices and are always looking for a bargain. Many stores manufacture their own goods so they can sell their own products for a good value to the consumer while still maintaining their margins. Department stores who used to buy all their goods from other manufacturers now make their own lines. Stores such as GAP manufacture their own clothing; Nordstrom and Eddie Bauer have their own labels as do many of the chain stores. We live in a very competitive retail environment.

Because of this, rep organizations have changed in recent times. It has been my experience to see many reps go out of business in recent years. The business of reping has changed with the times, and stores and manufacturers are not as dependent upon them as they used to be. Reps who used to depend upon department store business no longer can because the department store is manufacturing their own goods. This is not to say that you should not hire a rep, because often they can boost your business tremendously. You just must be careful about hiring the right one for you and your product and be very careful about monitoring or managing them. A sales rep represents your company and your product, so you better be careful about who they are.

WHAT YOU NEED TO KNOW ABOUT SALES REPS

As your business grows, you will need to find other people to sell your products not just yourself. You will find it is more economical for you to find independent sales representatives to sell for you because you will need more time for other parts of your business and you do not want to spread yourself too thin. One thing to remember is that *no one is ever as enthusiastic or knows your products as well as you do*. It is, therefore, up to you to create the enthusiasm in your sales rep and educate him or her about your product.

You need to remember that no matter what the rep tells you, the truth is his or her loyalty is to the retail store and not to your company. It sounds strange that, when you are the one signing their commission checks, they would not be loyal to you, but it simply does not work that way. The reason is, that the sales rep must keep his credibility with the retail store. They may purchase several lines out of the showroom and it is up to the rep to keep that customer happy. The last thing a rep wants to do is lose his customer by having him purchase goods that will not sell or buy the wrong quantities.

When you are ready to seek a sales rep, don't be disappointed if they don't fall all over you to get your line. Taking on a new line is called "pioneering" a line and not all reps want to do this. It takes lots of their time and energy to introduce a new company into the marketplace. Buyers are often skeptical of new lines because they have no track records for delivery, quality or sell through. Though reps are always looking for something new, they are often skeptical of someone new to the industry because — let's face it — they get paid when the goods are shipped and this is how they make their living.

Having often been asked " How do I find a good sales rep?" I've put together a few pointers first on where to find them and then, what to ASK them.

WHERE TO FIND A GOOD SALES REP:

Ask retail stores in the territory who they like working with and who they think would be a good rep to handle your product. If you already have customers in the territory with whom you do business, ask them first. If you don't do business in the territory find out who you'd like to do business with and then contact them and ask which sales reps they recommend. Many buyers have favorites that they enjoy working with and are happy to put you in touch with them. Just be sure this is a store where your line is already selling or a store where you'd really like to have your products.

Go to a Trade Center and visit Showrooms. Most major cities have trade centers where reps have permanent showrooms. These are showrooms where buyers purchase wholesale goods from all types of retail establishments. There is not necessarily access by the general public to these showrooms, so you will likely need to establish the purpose of your trip with a guard or some other official. Take proof that you are a legitimate business (business license, printed check forms, business cards etc., will usually do) because you may need to show proof that you have a business in order to get access. Once you are in the Trade Center go through various show rooms to see which reps carry what lines for sale. After careful observation you will be able to see which showrooms and which reps might best be able to represent your line. Don't look for lines that are exactly like yours, look for showrooms where your line would be complimentary. Be observant of how the sales people work in the showroom and if it's a small one, you can even talk to the rep. Be careful to respect the sales rep's time with paying customers.

Ask for referrals from other manufacturers: Your friends in the industry might be able to refer you to a rep they know.

Ask other sales reps: If you have found a showroom you like or rep you are impressed with and for one reason or another they are unable to take your line, by all means ask them for a referral. Often they will know a rep who is new to the business, looking for new lines and quite hungry to pioneer a new line. A referral from another rep can be a very good source for a new vendor. Remember, just because a rep is new does not mean he or she is not good, professional, honest and hard working.

Find out what other lines the rep has in his or her showroom. Are these direct competitors? Are they compatible with your line? You want your line to be different from other lines the rep has in his or her showroom so that you can make a statement.

WHAT TO LOOK FOR IN A SALES REP:

1. Ask The Following questions:
   - Employ due diligence: Call other vendors who are using this sales rep.
   - Has the sales volume met with their expectations?
   - Does the rep return phone calls and generally give good feedback?
   - Does the rep follow through with sales calls?
   - What is the rep's general reputation?
   - How long has the rep represented their line?
   - Is the rep hungry, meaning does he or she want and need to make a living?

2. **Interview the rep in person**. *Never, Never, Never* hire a sales rep without having a face to face meeting and seeing his or her showroom. Believe me, the worst thing you can do is give your product to someone you haven't met. You are entrusting this person to create significant sales volume for you and you are hiring this person to represent you and your company — You must meet!!! When you meet someone, you will develop rapport. The rep will see that you are serious about your business and you will be able to see if this is a person with whom you can develop a long term relationship.

3. **Check out the Showroom (unless the rep is a "road Rep") and look for the following :**
   ♦ Is the space well used?
   ♦ Is the showroom clean?
   ♦ Are the displays interesting and well merchandised?
   ♦ Ask how often displays are changed?
   ♦ Does the rep smoke? With the exception of some geographic areas, this is a real turn off to most buyers and your products will smell terrible. I would say do not hire a sales rep who smokes in the showroom. It simply alienates too many prospective buyers.

Once you decide on which rep to hire, then it is important to come to an understanding of what exactly you are hiring him or her to do for you. You will need to have a written agreement. Generally, it is not necessary to have a formal contract. Often a letter from you to the rep signed and acknowledged by both of you is sufficient. I am leary of the rep who presents you with a huge contract. I am not an attorney, so I cannot advise you as to the best agreement. However, it has been my experience that you both must come to an understanding of 3 elements: territory or where the rep can sell, commission rate, and when the commission will be paid. You may also include what you expect the rep to sell, but until you have had one or two seasons of experience with this rep, it is hard to predict.

How To Find A Store To Take Your Items On Consignment

You may decide that consignment is the way for your company to sell your product. When you sell on a consignment basis the store will put your goods up for sale at an established retail price and once the product sells, the store takes a percentage of the sale, (as stated earlier it is usually 40% to 60%), and gives you the rest. This is a good arrangement for the store because they do not have to buy your product directly, meaning they are under no obligation to purchase your product. If they have it in their store for awhile and it doesn't sell then they don't have to mark it down and lose money. They simply call you to come and pick it up. On the other hand, if it does sell then you both make a profit.

This can be a good way for you to obtain exposure of your product. Since the store is not under any obligation, they are often readily agreeable to putting your goods into their store if your product is a good fit with their other lines. It is also a good way for you to test the market with your product to see if your prices are right and your product is marketable. If you are a new vendor for the store, they can determine your credibility this way without the risk.

Art galleries and wearable art types of products are often in shops on consignment. I was recently visiting a store in a small resort area where they had magnificent products, both sewn products as well as other art, all from small companies. I spoke with the owner about how she worked — whether she bought on consignment or wholesale. Her answer was interesting. She told me that she had started her business six years ago and the way she financed it, in part, was by taking everything on consignment as she did not have to pay anyone unless the product sold. When the items did sell she paid the artist or manufacturer 50% of the retail sales price. Over the years, she made her store profitable to the point where she opened a second store (which, by the way, is also very profitable). Today, she purchases nearly all of her merchandise wholesale, taking only a few items on consignment. When those test out well in the retail market, she then purchases them at wholesale.

When you begin your search for a store to take your goods on consignment reread the section above on finding a sales rep. The store truly becomes your rep and you must find out all you can about that store's reputation and credibility before you allow them to market your product. It is best to begin your search for stores in your own geographic area. This way, you are comfortable about where your merchandise is. You can check on it once in awhile to see what progress is being made. You will really have an opportunity to test market your goods as you can change prices to see which ones are the best for your product.

A word of caution here about merchandising: This chapter has not touched on merchandising your products, but once you sell on consignment or if you rep your own line please be careful not to let a shop owner talk you into only displaying a few of your items. Make them take enough so your product makes a statement. You don't want your wonderful product to get lost in the store. Try putting together small displays of your goods and come up with a plan for showing the potential store how you think your products are best displayed to the potential buyers. Most store owners will welcome this information from you. If your items are sized, say you make womens blouses — you do not want a store to take only one blouse in one size on consignment, you want the store to take a least one of every size. On the other hand, if you make quilted pillows be sure you have a variety package of say a half dozen pillows that tell a story by being displayed together so the store owner can really market your company and your work.

When you work on consignment, even though you still own the product, be sure you have a written agreement stating; how long you will leave your goods there; when you expect payment after a sale; and who is liable for damage should your goods become shop worn, broken or otherwise destroyed. You do not want to wait until after the fact to establish these factors.

A different type of consignment is a product that is made especially for the customer — a personalized or custom product. The store might purchase one of your products and display it and then take orders — the Christmas stocking or personalized product , baby blankets, etc. You could leave one there and take orders or you could sell to them. It is always best to sell them the sample product but there are occasions where you might want to do otherwise. You could most likely talk anyone into doing this. They don't have to invest any money in the product, all they have to do is take orders and collect the money. You are actually producing samples and then taking orders directly from the end users.

Stores will often go for this arrangement. I can think of a few companies I know of who work very well in this manner. One is a woman who makes baby blankets that are personalized with the child's name and date of birth. A few samples are displayed in the store and the store also has a book with photographs of various designs that are offered. A customer selects the design they want and places an order with the specifics of the child's name and birth date. The store faxes the order to the manufacturer and the manufacturer makes up the order and sends it back to the store where the customer comes in and picks it up (another chance to sell something to that customer). The customer prepays for it, the manufacturer sends an invoice to the store and everyone is happy.

Some Alternatives to Reps & Consignment

There are many creative ways to sell your product besides the usual rep sales and consignment sales. These include sales to catalogs, direct marketing by mail order or your own web site or trunk shows. Here's a brief description of each.

Catalog Sales: There are many wonderful specialty catalogs in the market. You likely receive many of them yourself. These are excellent places to sell your products. They generally buy large quantities of each item and want delivery well in advance of a season with back up orders available if the item should sell well. Make a list of the ones you would like to be in — but DO NOT send them a sample. Contact the buyer and discuss your product. If it is something the buyer is interested in, then send a photograph along with your wholesale price list. Prices for catalog sales are always negotiable because the buyer wants the best deal possible and is generally willing to deal in quantities. Be prepared for them to ask for a discount off your wholesale price.

Direct Marketing: Some companies prefer to sell directly to customers by taking ads in magazines or selling via mailing lists. Cost of these ads can be very expensive depending on the publication, so be careful because there are no guaranteed sales. Consider the cost of the ad in your commission. Also, be prepared to pay for the ad regardless of your sales. There are many books on direct marketing and you might want to read a few of these before trying this method. If you do take out an ad, be prepared to receive requests from wholesalers who want to purchase your product on a wholesale level.

Web Sites/Cyber Stores: This is becoming so popular and is an excellent value as it is relatively inexpensive to create a web site. The trick here is to be able to be found by your potential customers. Even if you create a fabulous, innovative web site — it's only good if folks can locate you. It must be user friendly and you must have good graphics of your products. Remember this is similar to catalog sales, only you are selling directly to the consumer. If you are not an expert in this area I would suggest that you do lots of research before entering this market and hire a professional to help you.

Trunk Shows: This is actually a form of consignment. Specialty stores and even the better department stores love it when you come into their establishment for a day or so and display your products. You are there to answer questions from the public. If you have a particular skill, technique or way to demonstrate how the product is made, you can do it right on the spot so people can see and appreciate the process. Often, you will take items that are already complete and sell them directly or sometimes you can accept special orders to ship at a later date. In any case, the store only buys from you what is sold on those particular days. It is a good way to test market your product and get feedback from the customers. Even stores such as Price Club and Costco have a program where they do what they call roadshows. This is where a vendor sets up a display for a weekend and sells right from their own display — what a way to get sales! If you have a particular store in mind, ask about doing this.

Take the time and effort to research your pricing structure

Learning how to price for wholesale, retail, consignment or the consignment market is not brain surgery. It is best to make sure you take the time to research and plan your pricing. Know your target market, your competition and your costs. Plan and research the pricing just as you plan the rest of your products and business. It's worth the extra effort in the reward you will get when your products sell. Remember that your object is to sell your wares to make a profit — not just sell them at any price. Try to remove yourself from the emotional attachment you will likely have to your product and create a quality product that can be profitable. If need be, go back to the drawing board and change or redesign your product so your business is profitable and successful.

Buying Wholesale

Saundra Weed is extremely gifted as an entrepreneur (see Chapter 7 for more on Saundra Weed). Part of her success lies in the fact that she knows how to run her business. She is the expert on buying wholesale. In this chapter she shares her knowledge and contacts. Take note as Saundra shares her secrets:

What is wholesale buying anyway? "Wholesale" refers to buying large quantities of goods at a reduced or discounted price. You, the business owner, will then "resell" the goods at an inflated price, and collect sales tax. (Which will be paid quarterly or yearly to the State *Treasury* Department.) Buying wholesale is not the magic answer to making money from your business. Wholesale isn't always the cheapest price you can get. It helps, and sometimes buying wholesale helps a great deal. Making money is a combination of things:

- Pricing
- Location
- Customers
- Production
- Skill Level
- Supply and Demand
- Well-Planned Business Choices

Once you are a registered business, and have your tax I.D. number, you can purchase products in large quantities at discount prices of up to 50% off retail. Notice I said *up to 50%* and *large quantities,* as in bolts, boxes, dozens, and crates. Be careful! I've seen many new businesses end up with lots of inventory, but no cash flow.

A wholesaler will require a minimum order. That minimum order could be as little as $50 or as much as $1,000. The wholesaler might let you "split order," which means you can combine products, as long as they are full cases, to equal the minimum order. Do you really need a gross (144) of twenty-two inch white zippers? You will also be expected to purchase a certain dollar amount per year. If you do not meet their "dollar expectations," you will still be allowed to buy wholesale, but your "wholesale price" may only equal a 30% discount because of the small volume you purchase yearly.

Some wholesalers will only sell to you if you have a "store front" or "retail outlet." They make no provisions for home based businesses. *They don't want your business!* You are too small. Don't get bent out of shape. They've chosen their type of business the same way you've chosen yours. Respect their choice, and find a wholesaler who will do business with you.

Wait For Sales

Art stores, fabric stores and craft stores have lots of sales that are advertised well in advance. You may be better off buying *only what you need* at a 25% off sale price. You buy only what you want, in the colors you need, and your money is not tied up in extra stock. Now, I'm not talking about our fabric collections. We all have a great deal of money tied up in our *collections,* don't we?

Buy Direct

Consider buying direct from the manufacturer. Every packaged item has the manufacturer's name and state listed somewhere on the package. Write it down. Go to your library. There you will find a whole section with phone books. Find the state phone book and look up the phone number. Call them. Ask for a wholesale catalog or price list. Ask what their minimum order is. Don't flinch you don't have to place an order. You just want their catalogue and price list.

When is wholesale not wholesale?

After finding pearl buttons for $0.58 at a local discount store, I followed my own advice. I called the manufacturer and got the wholesale price, $0.70 ($0.12 more than the retail price at K-Mart). "Why?" I asked. "Because K-Mart orders large quantities of pearl buttons and has them carded especially for their stores," she answered. So I went to K-Mart for my buttons, which were cheaper than wholesale. End of story! I've included wholesale sources for your convenience, as well as tips on finding wholesalers. Just remember the following:

1. Check the price
2. Check the quantity you must purchase
3. Choose wisely

Finding Wholesale Suppliers

1. Start with trade magazines and publications.
2. Trade Shows—Sewing & Fabric (check the newspapers & magazines).
3. American Sewing Guild, and sewing, quilting and crafting associations
4. Ask other people.
5. Check the phone book by subject or related subject.
6. Check the 800# directory.
7. Look on the back of packages.
8. Once you've registered your assumed name you will receive all kinds of mail from wholesalers.
9. Check related wholesalers—Florist suppliers also carry lace, ribbon, beads, etc. Example categories: Fabric, Cleaners, Labels, Plastic bags, Beads.

Wholesalers List

❖ Checker Wholesale Distributors
   (419)-474-5434; 4343 Secor Rd., Toledo, Ohio 43623

❖ Meskin & Davis, Inc.
   (313)-554-2000; 14400 Woodrow Wilson, Detroit, Michigan 48238

❖ Jack Gells
   (313)-554-2000; 5700 Federal St., Detroit, Michigan

❖ Mac Enterprises
   (313)-846-4567; 5755 Schaefer Rd., Dearborn, MI48126

❖ Adam Barel Co.
   (800)-428-6311; 911 North E St., Richmond, IN 47374

Chapter 13

Mail Order List

- ❖ Clotilde - (800)-772-2891; notions, books, etc.

- ❖ Nancy's Notions - (800)-833-0690

- ❖ Many catalogues for fixtures, paper goods, dressmaking and tailoring supplies, etc.

Trade Shows

- ❖ Great Lakes Fabrics & Crafts Show - (216)-333-1300; P.O. Box 26289, Fairview Park, Ohio 44126

- ❖ Chicago Fabric 6 Trim Show - (312)-836-1041; for manufacturers, Merchandise Mart, Chicago, IL.

- ❖ Southeastern Fabrics, Notions and Crafts Association, Inc. -- Wholesale Buyers' Market in College Park, Georgia. Write to PO Box 937, Duluth, GA 30136

- ❖ New York International Fashion Fabric Exhibit - (212)-594-0880; Javitt Center, NYC, NY. Very large show, with seminars, latest technology, etc.

- ❖ Bobbin Show - (800)-845-8820; The "biggie" in Atlanta, GA. Especially good for larger manufacturers. All the latest for the industry, plus contract sourcing, seminars, hands-on demos, etc.

A Work Of Art

This picture is from Saundra Weeds creative sewing collection.

Picture courtesy of *Creative Images*

Is It Time For A Raise?

It is not enough that we have to agonize over our initial pricing structure—now we must make intelligent decisions regarding a raise! Just the mere thought of restructuring their pricing, catapults some sewing pro's into an instant state of panic. Pricing seems to be one of the more complicated issues for entrepreneurs. However, it need not cause you such grief. When considering a raise, ask yourself the following questions:

> **Am I charging what the market will bear?**
> **Has the demand for my services increased?**
> **Am I offering any new or additional services?**
> **Is my basic cost-of-doing business increasing?**

Factors You Should Consider

Each year you will experience an increase in some, if not all, of your cost-of-doing-business expenses. These increases must be accounted for in your pricing, thus eliminating any drain on your profit margin. Each year you should conduct a review of clients referred to you (client call sheet *), and your production logs (three month planners*). If they show a consistent increase in the demand for your services, this should be a clue that it is time to make some changes.

When you reach the point where you are virtually turning away business, you have several options: Hire employees, subcontract out work, or give yourself a raise. Let's say that you decide to give yourself a raise, consider the following:

In economics the rule of supply and demand prevails. More demand for a good or service, coupled with limited supply, will give rise to increased prices. For example, you have gained an excellent reputation as a sewing professional. You are only one of three in your community who specializes in home décor, and you now have more business than you can handle; the demand for your services has escalated. This is a good indicator that people would most likely be willing to pay more for your services.

Another valid consideration for giving yourself a raise is when you add new or additional services. Let's say that you took a special class that enabled you to offer new or additional services to your clients; you should be compensated.

So, what have we said thus far: You can consider giving yourself a raise if the cost of doing business increases; the demand for your services increases; you offer new services or increase your knowledge and skill level. These reasons in and of themselves are very good ones, nevertheless, how do you know if your clientele will object to increased prices? You must be diligent and conduct a market analysis to determine if there will be any price resistance, and more importantly you want to know what the market will bear.

QUIZ: In the last paragraph there were four reasons to give yourself a raise. Can you name all four?

"What The Market Will Bear!"

Keep in mind, some clients will complain no matter what. For them, it's a sport—they simply love to negotiate. Your job is to recognize what they are trying to do, and refuse to allow it to influence your decision making when it comes to your pricing policy.

There is a point at which you will receive some price resistance, and it is your responsibility to ascertain at what point this will occur. If you charge too much, you will have exceeded what the market will bear and your clients will let you know. Fear not, you can avoid this problem by conducting a market analysis.

Answer to quiz: You can consider giving yourself a raise if the cost-of-doing business increases; the demand for your services increases; you offer new services or increase your knowledge and skill level.

Testing The Market

Bianca, a seasoned sewing professional, was quite innovative in her research: She formulated a new price for the items on her price list. She selected various items from the list and utilized them as her test or market analysis. She designed and mailed a flyer to all of her existing clients. Her introductory paragraph was very strong, she reminded her clients of the services she offered and restated the convenience and value clients received by doing business with her. This is a good approach; it reaffirms in the clients mind why it is important to do business with you, and why you are valuable to them.

From her word processing software she selected some very elegant clip art of bedspreads, pillows, and draperies, and listed her *new* prices for each. She was very ingenious by pointing out the fact that during summer most people entertain out-of-town guests and recommended that they get a head start on sprucing up their homes.

The results of her test generated a twofold benefit: First, it confirmed that her clients had no objections to her price increase (most clients didn't even notice). Secondly, it gave her repeat bookings, and increased her profit margin as a result of her revised pricing policy. Bianca proves that deciding to give yourself a raise is easy when you know what the market will bear.

15

Do Banks Want To Loan Money To You?

Did you know that banks get report cards? That's right! They get graded on their ability to serve the credit needs of individuals in their community. They are literally required by law to meet the credit needs of the business community. The law was instituted in 1977—The Community Reinvestment Act (CRA).

It has been said that the law has favored women and minority owned businesses, however, banks are genuinely interested in loaning to entrepreneurs in general. The CRA mandates that banks be examined regularly and rated on their track record with respect to extending loans and credit to the community at large.

How Are Banks Rated?

♦ *Outstanding!*   ♦ *Satisfactory!*

At the time of my research, eight percent of the nation's leading banks had sustained an "outstanding" rating. A rating of satisfactory means that the bank needs improvement, or they simply have not met CRA compliance. There are penalties placed on banks for noncompliance. They aren't permitted to open new branches, and may not merge with another bank. With the varying economic climate, this could prove detrimental to a bank. It is to the benefit of the bank to get good ratings. In 1990, banks were required to make public their rating and performance evaluation. Request to see your bank's rating.

What are the advantages to you as a borrower to see a bank's ratings?

When you seek bank loans as a source of entrepreneurial financing, you want to find only those banks who are strongly committed to lending to entrepreneurs. If you have a good credit history and can demonstrate that you have a viable pay-back plan you should apply for a loan.

Start by listing known banks with a rating of "outstanding." Call to set an appointment to meet with the business banking officer. Ask them what their lending requirements are. Be sure to give the banking officer an overall picture of you and your business. Most importantly, let them know why you feel the additional capital will make a significant contribution to the growth and development of your business.

The number one rule when seeking financing, whether from a bank or any other lending institution, is to go prepared for your appointment. You will do so by making a list of what you need the money for. Ask yourself how would this extra money enhance your business. Do you need funds for inventory or business expansion? Be sure to take your business plan with you, the banking officer will be impressed to see how thorough you are. "Razzle-dazzle" them with your business savvy.

Most people are apprehensive when applying for loans—don't be. Remember the banking officer is there to help you and service the financial needs of the community!

16

Business Tools

Accounting

A number of sewing professionals expressed an interest in how to keep track of raw materials and finished goods in a simple, efficient manner. There are times when products may be moving so fast it could become an inventory tracking nightmare. However, with the advent of computers, a sound inventory tracking design and the right software program capable of bearing the brunt of the work, it will free you to do what you do best—make more money! But, which program do you use? How do you determine if it will make your life easier? The last thing you want to do is spend hundreds or thousands of dollars for a software package you can't even use.

In an effort to help clarify some of your options, I selected two of the most popular accounting packages on the market: Peachtree Accounting for Windows, and Mind Your Own Business Accounting (M.Y.O.B). My aim is to enable you to make an informed, intelligent decision when choosing a program to handle your business records. Due to the enormous amount of features, I focused on inventory tracking, maintenance, and auto-building or assembly. Auto-building or assembly is merely the process of taking raw materials and combining them into a finished product.

Mind Your Own Business Accounting, or M.Y.O.B. for short, was very user friendly and seemed oriented to the professional without a heavy accounting background. Highlight features include service items, service invoices, and different units of measure for buying and selling. Setting up only took a few minutes. Peachtree took a little longer to start up because you have to set up all the information for each section before you can effectively take advantage of the program. You'll also need to know some basic accounting to set it up correctly.

Tracking inventory

Each item has their own unique ID code. When assigning codes to items, group them by categories such as 123-THR. "-THR" would mean thread, so to list all thread you would tell the computer to look for all items ending in "-THR". In MYOB, unit prices can be entered up to three decimal places. If the item is to be sold, you just enter your profit margin (mark up percentage) and it figures the sale price for you. In both programs, a To Do List will alert which item levels are low so you can reorder what you need. Peachtree has three different methods for entering unit cost: Average, LIFO (last in, first out), and FIFO (first in, last out). Unit cost is recalculated every time you make a purchase if you use the Average Costing method. For example, you buy 3 yards of fabric for a $1 a yard, and another 3 yards at $2 a yard. The average cost would be $1.50 a yard. Peachtree also has up to 5 custom fields you can designate to describe anything you need to know about the item, but you cannot index the item by these fields.

Once the raw materials inventory was set up, I set out to create an assembled item. In MYOB you simply click an Auto-Build icon, highlight the items to use, enter the quantity, and MYOB does the rest. Whenever you sell that item, it will automatically update your inventory for you. Peachtree's method involves entering your components on a Bill of Materials. You can select whether to have all the components printed out on the invoice or not.

After reviewing both programs, I found the only distinct differences were in their presentations of basic concepts. However, MYOB is oriented toward a quick and easy style. Armed with the program that fits your style and needs, you can make sure nothing falls through the cracks. Hone your competitive edge with one of these programs in your arsenal of smart business tools.

Pricing Without Fear

Forms

Sewing for profit requires that you have forms to help you perform, complete projects and stay organized. Throughout this text we have referred to a number of forms regarding pricing for profit. We spoke of the forms offered by Collins Publications: The Complete Set of Forms and Forms on Computer Disk, the only difference is that the complete set of forms is hard copy forms, and the forms on computer disk are designed for customization on your personal computer. I thought it might be helpful to define the use of each form.

1. Business Policy: This form is used to define your policies, practices and procedures. It outlines what you require, such as deposits, consultation, late charges, etc.

2. Client Call Sheet: This form helps you screen new clients and track how clients are being referred to you. It ensures that you do not forget to tell them about your services, and reminds you to book the project and send your literature.

3. Request Form: Designed to save you time when clients are looking through pattern books. It serves to let you know what patterns clients like so that you can plan current and future projects for repeat business.

4. Project Worksheet: This form is used to calculate your labor and to avoid undercharging for labor intensive design details on projects.

5. Measurement Chart: It's important that you get each and every measurement correct; this form is essential in accomplishing your goal.

6. Pattern Adjustment Check List: It ensures accuracy on projects sewn by you, your employees or subcontractors. The form allows you to track production on clients' projects at each stage of development.

7. Why Custom Tailored Clothing: A sample marketing brochure using the subliminal approach to marketing, advertising and promotions for a sewing business. You may customize it to fit any sewing business.

8. Thank You Card: Sample used in many popular sewing businesses to show appreciation for clients who book projects and those who refer business to you. Referral leads taken from the Client Call Sheet data section.

9. Invoice: Designed specifically for those who collect deposits, charge labor, consultation, sell notions and fabrics. It also has a section for credits and taxes, with a balance due for pickup.

10-12. *Sample Price List 1,2, and 3: A 3-page price list illustrating charges derived from the integrated pricing method. You build specific categories in order to price your goods and services for profit.

13. Consultation Work Agreement: This is a sewing industry standard contract for pricing your labor and consultation fees. It has a section for figures derived from the Project Worksheet and a section for added design details. There are sections for initial interviews, fittings and pickup appointments. Also used for Business Policy documentation and it is used to make your invoice. One of the most important forms you will ever use!

14. Consignment Agreement: A contract designed for sewing professionals who desire to place their items into retail establishments on consignment. It spells out who is responsible for all facets of the contractual agreement.

15. Pricing Sheet: This form is used to calculate labor, fabric and notions used to place items into retail establishments, sell wholesale to stores or to price items made for display. It has a section to prepare your hang-tag and track where the finished item will be placed.

16. Employment Application: The only application designed for the sewing industry for hiring employees or subcontractors. All questions are designed to determine sewing knowledge and expertise.

17. Independent Contractors Agreement: Once you have decided to subcontract out work on your projects you need to have a contract that stipulates your policies, practices and procedures and who is liable for all facets of production. This form is designed to accomplish that goal.

18. Sewing Lessons Contract: This contract is designed for teaching either private or groups sessions. It also allows you to obtain parental permission for teaching minors.

19. Sewing Class Rules/Regulations: This form stipulates your policies, practices and procedures and who will be liable for all facets of the teacher-student relationship.

20. Time and Motion Chart: This is the tool used to determine true production time. To keep the study pure you start the clock and stop it whenever you receive an interruption or take a break. Although you may be performing your study on a unit, you will derive the small labor intensive design details (items) needed for your miscellaneous column on your price list. These are such things as buttons, hook and eyes, snaps, zippers, matching stripes and plaids, and anything you think will be an item pricing element on your final price list. We need to know production time for construction as both an item and a unit for pricing our labor.

21. Price List Worksheet: This is the last form needed to develop your final price list. You will take the figures from the "total time column" of your time and motion chart and put them in the column labeled "total time" on your price list worksheet. Once you have all the labor figures for items as well as units, you will use your base hourly rate to figure your labor charges

22. Inventory Sheet: Used to track items placed into retail establishments on consignment, in fashion shows or placed in your studio for promotions. Often used in conjunction with Pricing Sheet and Consignment Agreement.

13. Project and Task List: Used to list all of the labor elements that you perform on your projects. You will list them in three categories: Initial Preparation; Construction, both as an item and as a unit; We want item figures so we can charge for small labor intensive design details when needed; and Finishing. These are all the tasks preformed to get the project ready for completion. Some professionals place pick-up time in this section. Those who specialize in home décor might put their installation time here.

     * These forms can be found in the Complete Set Of Forms or Forms on Computer Disk, see the order form at the end of this book.

Complete Set of Form and Forms On Computer Disk

Form #	Form Name	Form #	Form Name
__ 1	Business Policy	__ 13	Consultation Work Agreement
__ 2	Client Call Sheet	__ 14	Consignment Agreement
__ 3	Request Form	__ 15	Pricing Sheet
__ 4	Project Worksheet	__ 16	Employment Application
__ 5	Measurement Chart	__ 17	Independent Contractors Agreement
__ 6	Pattern Adjustment Check List	__ 18	Sewing Lessons Contract
__ 7	Why Custom Tailored Clothing	__ 19	Sewing Class Rules/Regulations
__ 8	Thank You Card	__ 20	Time and Motion Chart
__ 9	Invoice	__ 21	Price List Worksheet
__ 10	*Sample Price List 1	__ 22	Inventory Sheet
__ 11	*Sample Price List 2	__ 23	Project Task List
__ 12	*Sample Price List 3		

Working Efficiently Helps Increase Your Profit Margin

So far we have discussed how to price for profit, however utilizing your time wisely also affects your profit margin. *Saundra Weed* has some excellent suggestions on how to accomplish that goal:

In order to work efficiently and make your time as valuable as possible, I suggest you do three things:

1. Eliminate time wasters.
2. Eliminate interruptions and distractions.
3. Use production methods.

Eliminate Time Wasters

1. Set aside a work time for orders.
2. Make sure you have *all* the supplies before you start. This should be done several days before you start the project. Having to stop in the middle of a project because you don't have the right thread, paint, or fabric – you name it, is one of the *biggest* time wasters. By the time you go out and buy it, you've lost valuable production time and created a rush job.
3. Another time waster is hunting for *lost tools*. Have two sets of tools and clean up after each project. Put things away so you can find them when you begin the next project.

Chapter 16

Eliminate Interruptions

1. Set aside regular work hours and keep them.
2. Use an answering machine, return calls later.
3. Post a sign on your door. *Working Do Not Interrupt.*
4. If you have children use a timer or an alarm clock. Promise them that you will read to them in 30 min. Set the timer for the agreed upon time. *Keep your promise!* Allow them to do the same when you interrupt them. Let them say, "I'll do it in ___ min. / hr. and set the timer. Life becomes more pleasant.
5. "_____" fill in your own interruption. What is your creative solution?

_____

My design time is very precious to me. One interruption could cost me a days work. From my personality checklist, I've already determined that I'm a "feast or famine" type of person. I prefer to work from 10 a.m. to 4 p.m. with no breaks and no lunch. I break from 4 p.m. to 6 p.m. and then work from 7 p.m. to 10 p.m. That's the way I like it. When I'm "on a roll," I can work till 2 a.m. and not be tired. I prefer to work long and hard, and take the next day off. On a work day I do not: Answer the phone, cook, visit with friends, do errands, etc.

How do you like to work? What are your comfortable work hours? Can you work with company? Do you like to work alone? My friend Nancy has people coming in and out of her studio all day long. She fields a million phone calls, on her portable phone, while she continues to sew her quilts. And she never misses a beat. She is truly amazing. I need quiet and concentration. What do you need?

Use Production Methods

The use of production methods will increase your "dollar" value per hour. Don't eliminate quality for the sake of speed. But, don't eliminate speed just because you don't know how to increase your output: take a class; buy a video; buy a book on shortcut sewing; study with a pro; or use advice from your networking friends.

Production Tips

   · Use rotary cutters to speed up cutting time
   · Commercial sewing machines sew faster than domestic models
   · Learn to cut without pinning
   · Learn to sew without pinning

Increase Your Income By Increasing Your Production and Skill Levels!

17

Developing Your Workspace

I have had the opportunity to do the design and layout for a number clients needing space plans. I have designed sewing studios as well as plans for commercial office buildings. Of course, the one I enjoyed the most was designing my own personal sewing studio, which is on the cover of my book, *The "Business" Of Sewing*. Since I covered in detail how I designed the layout for both my office and my studio in that book, I felt it would be exciting to explore how other sewing professionals have designed theirs. First Saundra Weed will give us some helpful guidelines for designing a number of workspaces as Bonnie L. Motts shares her expertise for developing a sewing studio. To complete the picture, Anita Greene shows us that studio expansion can be manageable and rewarding.

Setting Up A Sewing Studio— What will you need?

Equipment	Space	Special Equipment	Storage

Sewing Machine
  Kind
  How many
Sergers
  Kind
  How many
	Office
	Design Area
	Sewing Area
	  Machine Sewing
	  Hand Sewing
	Cutting Area
	Hanging Area
	Pressing Area
	Packaging Area
	Fitting Area
		Commercial
		Blind Hemmer
		Beading
		Quilting
		Other
		Iron
		Ironing Board
		Clothing Rack
		Mirror/s
		Scissors (kind)
		Rotary Mat
			Fabrics
			Finished Products
			Patterns
			Supplies
			Back-up Equipment
			Special Lighting
			Desk
			File Cabinet
			Dress Forms

Do you want the look of a professional workroom or do you want a professional working room?

I have two adjoining studios separated by a door. Each is approximately 18 by 23 feet. One is for sewing. One is for painting. My fitting room and office are upstairs, so the client never enters my work area unless they are invited into that space. My studio is very pleasant. It has paneled walls, almost entirely covered by white pegboard, and a white floor. There are two cutting tables, four sewing machines, two sergers, two irons (at opposite ends of the room), and one tabletop pressing unit. I also have floor to ceiling shelves everywhere for books, lace, and bolts of fabric. I choose not to see customers in my workspace for the following reasons.

1. I design wedding gowns and wearable art. My white fabrics need to stay white with no fingerprints, ballpoint pen marks, lipstick, or spilled coffee. All of those things that can accidentally happen while customers browse.
2. Accidents can happen! There are pins all over the floor of my workroom, as well as hot irons, fabric paints, etc. Need I say more?
3. The expensive computer sewing machine is the reason you need to keep people out of your work area. You know what else happens when people see your equipment ... they want *free* lessons ... like "Which machine do you like best and why?" or "What kind of feet do you use?" or "How does this work?"

For those reasons I maintain a workroom where I cut, sew, and create alone (and am free to throw things on the floor). My solution to keeping customers out of my former work space in my dining room sewing center was through the use of a folding screen. I simply refinished the wood and made new fabric panels to match my decor. There are simple directions available at your sewing and hardware stores for making your own fabric screens. In another home where my sewing area had expanded into a dining room and sun porch area I used two bookshelves side by side. I hung white peg boards on the back of the shelves. This became both a divider and a showcase. The white peg board was the perfect display area for my paintings and art garments.

My workspace also includes an upstairs bedroom for my fitting room. This room is ideally situated at the top of a stairway and next to a bathroom. Customers do not walk through my home. They are greeted at the door. Clothing to be altered is hung on a special over the door clothes hanger. Customer's coats and hats are hung in the closet. We proceed up the stairs to the fitting room. I fit wedding gowns with long trains so my fitting room must be large. It is also decorated in shades of white, ivory, pale gray, and pink. My fitting room must look clean, airy, and professional at all times. I've also chosen to decorate it in a feminine manner with vases of flowers and French Provincial furnishings and full length mirrors.

Finding Space for Your Business

The amount of space you have available in your allotted work area will have a definite impact on the kind of sewing business you can successfully run at this time. If you only have a *corner* of the bedroom, start with alterations. If you have a *whole* bedroom you have more options. Choosing a compatible business that fits into the space you have available now will make you money. It doesn't matter what size the room or what kind of equipment you have, You Can Start A Sewing Business NOW! !

The Dining Room Table

This requires constant set up and take down time, unless you can convince your family to eat on TV trays until the project is completed. Everything is done on the table space: cutting, sewing, gluing, packaging, etc. Amazing things have been accomplished by "creative sewers" in this alternate work space.

A Remodeled Closet / Laundry Room / Corner of Bedroom

This is a crafter's delight. You can actually close a door and leave "stuff" out on the cutting table or sewing machine. These spaces can be very efficient, as long as you keep your projects small and have good lighting. Dolls, toys, tote bags, children's clothes, wearable art, quilts, can all be created in this small space. This space will also accommodate a full-size alteration business or design studio.

A Real Studio

This space is going to be different for each person. It's a Dream—the studio we picture in our heads for the future. But you need to keep track, on paper, of what the ideal sewing space would be, or have in it to make you happy. Sometimes that environment can be achieved in the space you already have. Maybe you just need a little creative remodeling.

For example, you like to look out the window, but your sewing space is in the basement facing a blank wall. Could you hang up a painting of a landscape or flowers? Or take a photo of a view you love and have it blown up to poster size, framed, and hung where you can look out the "window wall" and still see your favorite outdoor scene while you are sewing? Doing this really made a difference in my mood while sewing. Or maybe you'd like to face a design wall while you are working, or see a wonderful assortment of fabrics stacked from floor to ceiling, arranged by color. Still have a fabric collection? I like to look at it for inspiration.

A Store

"Someday I want to own a store!" This is a statement I hear from many of you. Do more of what you're doing. Save a little more along the way. Before you know it ... your dream will come true.

Begin Your Design

Start by creating a work flow chart for yourself. Do you naturally *move* from left to right or right to left? Set up your workroom to accommodate that natural flow. Life in your workspace becomes more pleasant using this process.

- Do you need to press as you sew?
- Do you need an island area?
- Can your sewing machine face the wall?
- Do you *need* to look out of a window?
- Are you making small items? Or large?
- Are you making drapes, or wedding gowns, or quilts? (an island area with a sewing machine at one end is a must for this type of sewing)
- Where will you sit to sew?
- Is it comfortable?
- What do you want to look at while you sew? TV, window… painting?
- Need to hang as you sew?

Use the information on your "equipment page" to design your sewing room layout. There are many good books out that can help you plan a comfortable work area. Check your library and sewing store for these. For me what works is moving the furniture around and working in that space until it feels right. It usually takes *me four* tries before I feel comfortable with the flow. I'm a visual person, sometimes those little squares and rectangles that are cut out of colored paper, and then moved around on graph paper until they fit, don't always work for me. Although the furniture will fit into the room, I can't envision how *tall* things will be. If furniture is too tall, I sometimes feel cramped and blocked in; a trapped feeling.

Don't forget about good lighting. Good lighting can make a small space very comfortable. You don't have to hire an electrician. Just buy some "shop lights," or even a clip-on will help. Here are some suggestions on setting up a Sewing Center that will work in almost any size room, large or small. Before I give you the directions/instructions to create, "Saundra's Instant Sewing Room," let's do a little *thinking on paper*.

Thinking on paper saves me lots of time and money. I highly recommend trapping all your ideas on paper and keeping them in your workbook or business notebook. You will need to develop a flow chart for yourself before you begin to design your work space. On paper, list your ideal work situation. By writing down the steps it takes to start and finish a project you will get *a feel* for making your work space very comfortable. For example, A bride cannot try on a wedding gown by changing in the bathroom—you will need a large fitting room with mirrors. You get the idea. Start at the very beginning of a project and list the steps it will take to reach completion.

For example:
✂ An alteration business starts in the fitting room.
✂ A home decor business may actually start at the customer's home.
✂ A craft business might start at a flea market and need a lot of storage space.
✂ A production business may need a little or a lot of space, depending on what you are making.

Setting Up a Sewing Studio/Workspace

My friend Nancy has a studio *"to die for"* but she still rearranges it *constantly* to suit her needs. That came as a big surprise to me. I was looking for the ideal set up, the one that looked like *Better Homes and Gardens.* Yes, the sewing room nobody uses, the sewing room you just take "pictures" of. Listen carefully, these next words will save you a great deal of aggravation. *There is no perfect sewing room! None—Nada!*

You will constantly be rearranging it to make it better. There now, doesn't that make you feel better? A perfect workspace doesn't even have to be in one room or even on one floor. Many sewing professionals find it more convenient to have several rooms in different locations to operate their business from.

Once Again. Make a List. Think on paper.
- ❑ **What** space do you need?
- ❑ **Why** do you need it?
- ❑ **Where** do you need it?
- ❑ **How** do you get it?
- ❑ **When** do you need it-- all the time, part time, once a week/month ?

Work Racks and Storage

Clear Plastic Boxes (Large Size)

Used to hold customer's fabric, notions, patterns, instruction sheet, etc. (After the order is cut and folded it is put back in the "Work Box" until I'm ready to complete the order.) Another box holds the headpiece supplies. These same size boxes are used, in other areas, to store interfacings, assorted trims, and experimental sewing samples.

Suspended Racks

These can be used in the closet or laundry room for storage of extra hangers, fabric, etc. You can make them yourself. This is a really easy project. You will need:

- ➤ Two 12-inch pieces of chain (the hardware store will cut them for you)
- ➤ One old broom handle with broom end or a drapery rod.
- ➤ Measure the broom handle or rod by holding it up to the ceiling and seeing where the beams are.
- ➤ Insert one cup hanger in each beam approximately 8 to 10 inches in from the end of the rod.
- ➤ Slip 2 ends of the chain over the cup hook to form a loop.
- ➤ Slip the rod or broom handle through the loops.
- ➤ Voila! Instant clothes rack.

Garment Racks

Clothes or garment racks have a zillion uses. I own six. Three are always in use, and three are backups.

Rack #1

Is used in the cutting area for hanging fabric slopers (my own custom designed and hand drafted patterns) and cut garments. Or else, garments ready for "re-cuts," my term for a garment that has been fitted and now needs to be re-cut to a different size or shape because the customer has lost or gained weight. Hint: If you are using tissue patterns reinforce them with one-sided fusible webbing that can be ironed on.

Rack #2

Is in the fitting room and has been built up to allow extra height for wedding gowns to be hung. You could also raise the bars in your regular closet, which I have also done.

✂ Clothes in the closet are ready for pickup (pressed, stuffed with tissue, and bagged).

✂ Others are ready for a fitting and marked with the day, date, and time of the fitting appointment.

Rack #3

This rack is used in the sewing room for "Work in Progress." It holds garments that are at both the *beginning* and *ending* of their sewing lives. In other words, if it needs anything at all that must be *sewn* it is on this rack. I always know where I can find it. To make things even easier I have also taken index cards, into which I've cut a circular hole, to use on the rack as daily work dividers. Note: If you only sew two days a week, divide your rack into two. (The divisions match sewing days.) And, while I'm at it, let me remind you to put a red dot next to the customer's name on your calendar when you finish their order. Then, if the customer calls to check on an order you can tell at a glance if it's been completed. Train your hired help to use the same "red dot" system. This way, time is not lost looking for completed orders. You'll know it is aging on the "Done" rack, ready for pickup.

The Other 3 Racks

They are used for:

✂ Fashion shows

✂ Cleaning out the closet

✂ Display or Photography.

✂ Sorting and labeling sample clothing for lectures

✂ Fabrics I am creating by dyeing, manipulating, or embellishing.

✂ Designing or testing groups of fabric colors to see if I like them together.

Choosing Your Ideal Shaped Space

Make a list of all the activities that will take place in your studio space.

❖ Cutting

❖ Sewing

❖ Pressing

❖ Storage

❖ Packaging

A small space—Ideal for a one person business for:

❖ Alterations

❖ Crafts

❖ Doll making

❖ Designing/layouts

❖ Making samples

The "M" shape—Ideal for the single sewer with multiple sewing areas:

❖ Cutting

❖ Sewing

❖ Pressing

❖ Serging

The "M + "L"—Ideal for two workers
The "L" shape—Ideal for the single worker
The "T" shape—Ideal for two workers
* See illustrations that follow.

The "Island"—Ideal for:
❖ Cutting
❖ 2 sewers
❖ Large projects (such as draperies, quilts, wedding gowns, coats)

1. BAR OR ISLAND

against wall

OR

Free standing

The Shape of Your Space

There are really only *five* good setups for any work area. It doesn't matter what kind of work you do. All offices and work spaces are just variations on a theme. They are:

1. The Wall Unit:
2. The "L" Shape:
3. The "T" Shape:
4. (a) The "M" Shape: (b) The "M" with Island:
5. The Free Standing Island:

The Best Setups:

2. "L" SHAPE

in corner

facing interior

3. "T" SHAPE

1. Bar or Island
2. "L" Shape
3. "T" Shape

4B. "M" SHAPE WITH ISLAND

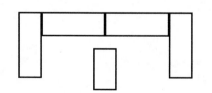

4A. "M" SHAPE

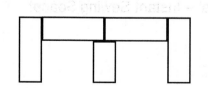

**Note: Diagrams 3, 4A, 4B, and 5
Are good setups for two or more workers.**

5.

Table

—— **Sewing Machine**

Recipes For "Saundra's Instant Sewing Centers"

These can be small, but are very efficient and "cheap." They can be set up almost anywhere; against a wall or as an island. You can put up a folding screen in front of it when company's coming, or throw a tablecloth over it and use it as a buffet for parties. It is easily assembled and knocked down (for storage when necessary).

Instant Sewing Center For A Small Spaces

See illustrations of diagrams on the next page.

Diagrams 1 & 2

Ingredients: (see diagrams 1 & 2)
❖ 1 door (any flat surface)
❖ 2 file cabinets
❖ 4 free cardboard egg boxes (from the grocery store)

Diagram 3

Instructions: Place in sequence (see diagram 3)
❖ 2 stacked egg boxes
❖ 1 filing cabinet
❖ leave a space
❖ 1 filing cabinet

Diagram 4

Add: (see diagram 4)

❖ 1 hollow core door balanced on top of the boxes or filing cabinets serves as the tabletop.
❖ Fill drawers with sewing notions, patterns, pressing equipment.
❖ Extra fabrics, etc., go in the egg boxes.
   Voila' – Instant Sewing Space!

Saundra's Instant Sewing Centers

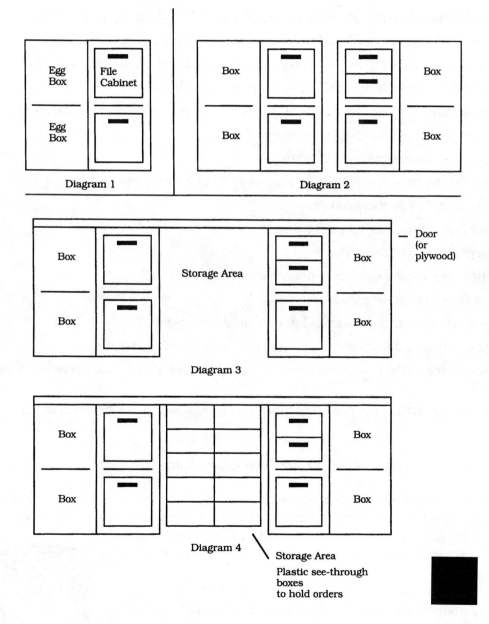

Egg Box
File Cabinet
Egg Box
Diagram 1
Box
Box
Box
Box
Diagram 2
Box
Box
Storage Area
Box
Box
Door (or plywood)
Diagram 3
Box
Box
Box
Box
Diagram 4
Storage Area
Plastic see-through boxes to hold orders

Planning A Sewing Studio

Bonnie L. Motts is a couture designer and dressmaker, and owner of *Bon's Place "Your Total Image Studio.* She is also a professional image consultant, fashion coordinator, skin care specialist, and make-up artist, to men, women, and teens. Bonnie offers some very helpful suggestions on designing a studio that is functional and productive.

When planning your studio, consider the following:

- Custom furniture, or units that can be interchanged, and an office chair on wheels.
- Shelves behind doors for fabrics. Drawers for patterns, lining, interfacing, notions.
- Heights that will work well for your body to eliminate fatigue when you cut or iron.
- Where you will hang your finished and work-in-progress items.
- Have separate tops that can connect from one unit to another unit for more flexibility.
- Don't forget your bookcases for your library of books.
- Where you will store *large* bolts of fabric.
- A separate ironing table top that can be removed and placed anywhere.
- Trash receptacles! (You will need plenty).
- Your customer entrance and dressing area.
- Where to place the bathroom area!
- Your office area and the number of phones needed.
- Customer file cabinets for easy access.
- Where you will hold your pattern and design consultations.
- Where you will store and display your retail products if you carry them.
- Color choices for walls, floors, and counters, as well as decorative accessories for accent.

**Bon's Place Sewing Studio: The following two pages have illustrations of layout and design.

Bon's Place "Your Total Image Studio

I chose a neutral taupe embossed paper for the walls and the windows are dressed with taupe mini blinds and a valance designed in a geometric pattern. I selected a commercial grade of carpet in a color that would blend with my home interiors. It's a diamond pattern design in colors of old fashion rose, taupe, and brown with a small touch of blue in what looks like a flower.

The cabinets are custom made in birch wood stained like a maple finish, which matches the paneling on one wall. Paneling was also used as wainscoting around the other 3 walls with wallpaper above the wainscoting. We built movable units that were made to look as if they were built in. The backs were finished so that they could be moved anywhere in the room, and they contained deep drawers to allow for plenty of storage.

Bon's Place "Your Total Image Studio"

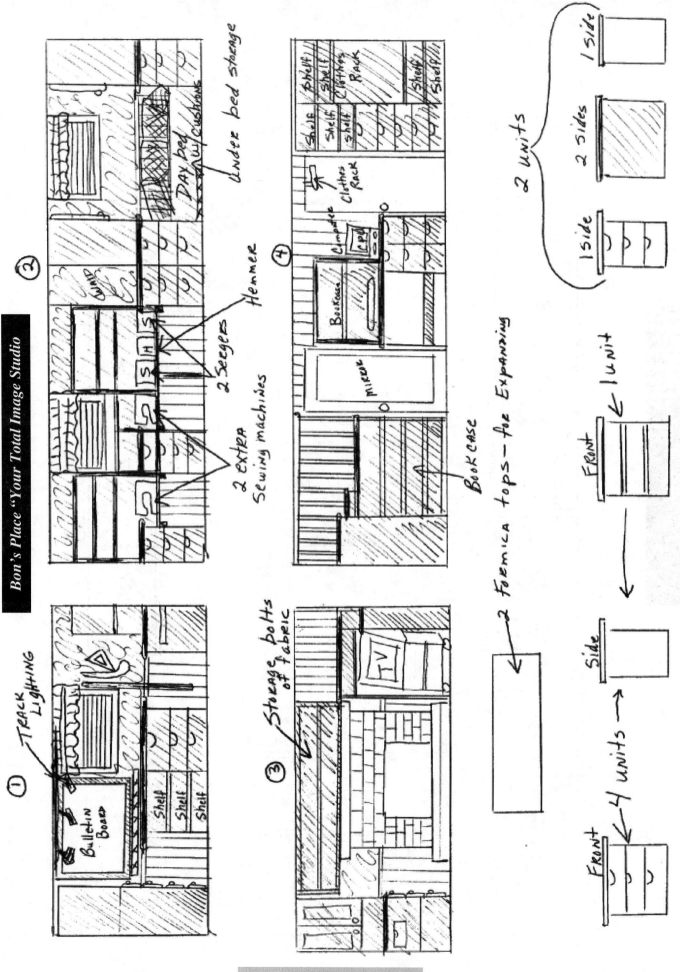

① TRACK LIGHTING
Bulletin Board
Shelf
Shelf
Shelf

② Sink
Day Bed w/ Cushions
Under bed storage
2 Serger
Hemmer
2 Extra Sewing machines

③ Storage bolts of fabric
TV

④ Shelf / Shelf / Clothes Rack / Shelf / Shelf
Shelf / Shelf / Shelf
Clothes Rack
Computer
CPU
Bookcase
Mirror
Book Case

2 Formica tops—for Expanding

1 Side   2 Sides   1 Side
2 units

Front   1 unit

Side
Front   4 units

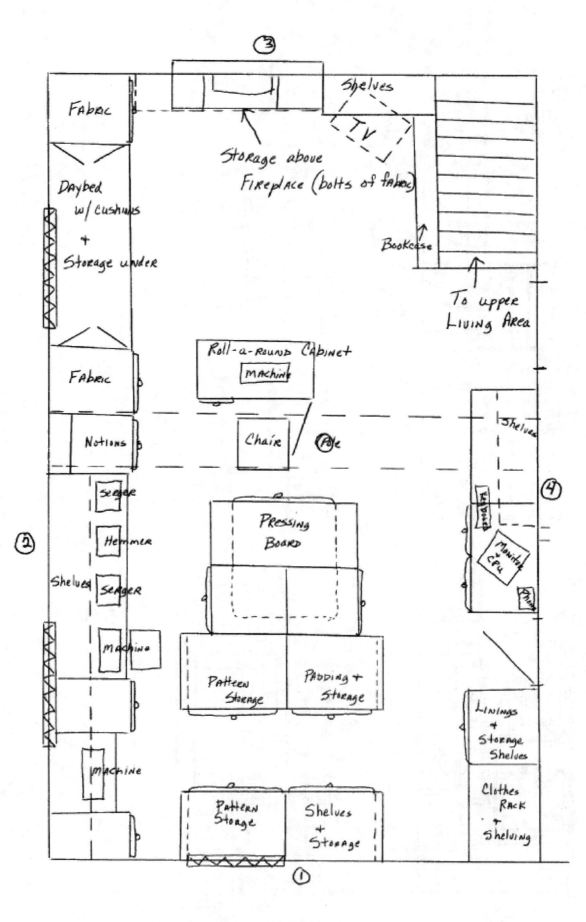

Bon's Place "Your Total Image Studio"

③

Fabric

Daybed
w/ cushions
+
Storage under

Fabric

Notions

②

Shelves

Seager

Hemmer

Seager

Machine

Machine

Shelves

Storage above
Fireplace (bolts of fabric)

Bookcase

To upper
Living Area

Roll-a-round Cabinet

Machine

Chair

Pole

Pressing
Board

Pattern
Storage

Padding +
Storage

Pattern
Storage

Shelves
+
Storage

①

Keyboard

Monitor
+ CPU

Printer

④

Linings
+
Storage
Shelves

Clothes
Rack
+
Shelving

The units that I have in the middle of the room were made to be used for pressing, design, and cutting. I'm 5'4" and the units were 33" inches high, not counting the pressing board on top or the extra bridge boards. The height should be according to comfort for less fatigue. A separate pressboard was made with muslin and wool padding. Formica was used on the bridge board units that housed my sewing machines and computer. The other units were done with wood tops because I could cover them with the bridge boards and pressboard. I added outlet strips all over for convenience. I also added fluorescent lights and spotlights. The area looks nice with plants and greenery to give it a warmer feeling and provide consistency with the rest of the house. I also had two large 2' x 7' free-standing boards made to lie side-by-side, or to lie separately depending on the way my room was set up. They can be used to bridge across units to provide additional space for machines or cutting space. There are two other units that were added to fit under the large bridge board along the wall where my four machines are located. Each unit has one large drawer and one shelf, which are movable.

Studio Expansion — Manageable and Rewarding *

A studio expansion, especially one that involves remodeling a personal residence, can be a big undertaking. However, it needn't overwhelm you if you plan carefully and anticipate your future needs. Anita Greene of NiNi Designs agrees. She served as general contractor for a project that involved an addition to her home to accommodate her dream studio. "Don't let the idea of expanding your studio or home office intimidate you. It's simply a matter of planning and being well-organized. I want beginning and intermediate seamstresses to know that they can expand their workspace areas economically."

Anita took charge of the three-month project, hiring the architect, the subcontractors and overseeing the construction. Starting from literally the ground up, she supervised the pouring of the foundation, all the way to designing custom cabinetry for her sewing equipment, modular office equipment and closet organizers.

Planning for the project actually started with a sketch of her dream studio six years prior. "I brainstormed about all the features that would make an ideal professional studio. 'Wouldn't it be great' I thought to myself 'if the studio had a separate entry from a major street with a rock pack leading up to it, and two windows facing the street?' " And that's exactly what she set out to achieve for herself. After three years of working out of a couple of back bedrooms, Anita had outgrown her workspace and was eager to build an addition to her home that would house her dream studio. "I wanted a professional sewing studio that would project a serious business image, and I really wanted to preserve my family's privacy in our home."

That decision made, she began her planning. "It's unbelievable the amount of research that I put into designing my studio," she said. "But then, that's how I approach everything that I do. I talked with everyone I could. At PACC meetings, I would ask my colleagues to let me know about any feature in their studios that they particularly appreciated. I visited several different sewing studios to take pictures, along with copious notes."

She also consulted with professional studio designer Lynette Ranney Black on the layout to make sure she hadn't overlooked anything. "Lynette helped me to plan furniture and equipment placement for optimum work flow, and advised me to add direct task lighting," Anita stated.

After the studio layout was planned, the next step was to hire an architect. "Designing the addition to our home was a challenge," Anita noted. "I wanted to make sure the studio was an investment that would enhance the future resale value of our home, while incorporating it in a way that would blend with the existing lines of the house."

While the architect drew up the plans for the 840-square-foot addition, Anita began lining up subcontractors for each phase of the project. "As the general contractor, I had to interview a number of professionals from plumbers to electricians, and then try to make the best choice I knew how," she explained. "Fortunately, I had a brother-in-law in construction who did my framing and roofing. It really pays to take advantage of personal connections to make sure you're getting someone who does good quality work at a fair price."

Once the architectural plans were finalized, the pace quickened. "There was a lot to orchestrate," she stated. "I had to apply for building permits, schedule subcontractors, select and purchase building materials, and arrange the mandatory inspections at each stage of building before the next stage could be initiated."

Surveying her studio today, Anita said the planning and hard work was worth it. "My work days go so much smoother now that everything is laid out and organized to accommodate the most productive work flow and to reduce physical strain," she reported.

Her sewing machines are built into the modular cabinets for ease of use, efficiency and to provide ample workspace. The nearby electronic serger is used to construct and finish garments. Overhead, a 200-cone serger thread rack and a 110-cone thread rack reflect a rainbow of colors.

Her cutting table is actually a refinished wooden drafting table with a series of wide flat drawers organized to hold everything from scissors and rotary cutters to an endless array of notions. Topped with a gridded, self-healing rotary mat, the cutting table also has a sturdy metal rod on one end that holds large fabric bolts, allowing Anita to reel out fabric as she cuts out patterns.

Along one wall is another wooden island topped with a heated, reflective pad for ironing, with pattern drawers underneath that can easily store over a thousand patterns. Anita added a separate electrical outlet switch within easy reach to make ironing that much easier.

A display rack showcases her latest designs, ranging from sporty windbreakers and ski jackets to cardigans and stirrup pants. A generously sized, full-length beveled mirror flanks a closet with attractive wood folding doors that reveal fabric hung neatly on hangers. Across the room, a walk-in fabric pantry with shelves accommodates a colorful display of fabrics and countless pattern books for clients to browse through for ideas. It also serves as a dressing room.

Another corner contains an L-shaped computer workstation. The desk accommodates her computer monitor and keyboard, with shelves overhead for manuals and drawers underneath for business files. With this setup, there's room for her printer, paper supplies and even more manuals.

Ergonomically designed chairs and good lighting ensure top productivity and comfort. Four large overhead fluorescent lights provide ample general lighting. Eight recessed lights with Alsaec reflects are controlled separately to furnish direct task lighting over her sewing machines. Three large windows (with pleated shades that can be drawn for customer privacy) provide plenty of natural lighting as well.

A separate outside entrance to the studio features a well-landscaped rock pathway leading up to the doorstep. An outdoor sign on a fence facing the street calls more attention to the two studio windows that showcase her latest creations.

Anita cautioned anyone considering building or remodeling a studio to anticipate their future equipment needs and changing conditions. "I've bought more equipment and recently hired a subcontractor to work with me, and it's still very comfortable. We have five different workstations, plus the computer workstation, so we don't have to worry about tripping over one another.

The studio reflects Anita's knack for exacting detail without losing sight of the overall effect. "It may have taken me a little longer to build the studio myself, but I got exactly what I wanted."

Studio Expansion by Ann Jansen, reprinted courtesy of Collins Publications.

STUDIO LAYOUT

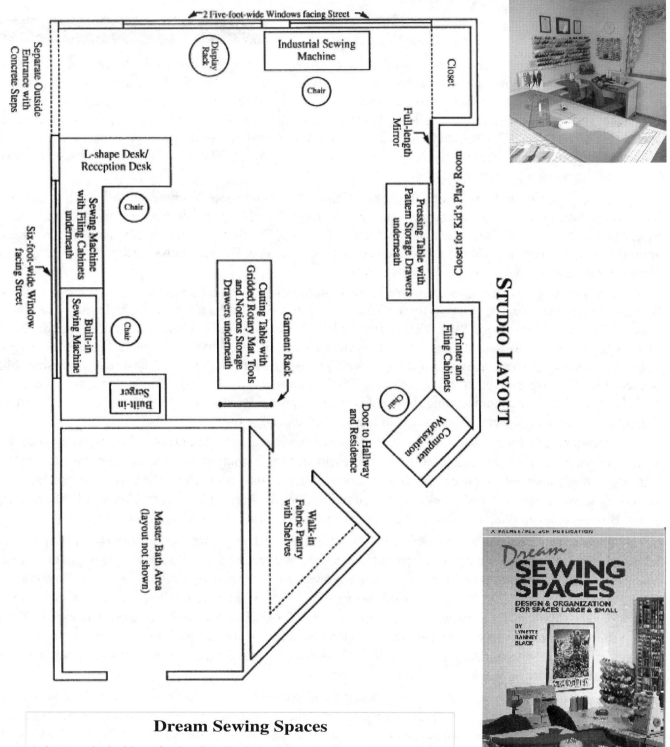

2 Five-foot-wide Windows facing Street

Separate Outside Entrance with Concrete Steps

Six-foot-wide Window facing Street

Display Rack

Industrial Sewing Machine

Chair

Closet

Full-length Mirror

Closet for Pr's Play Room

L-shape Desk/ Reception Desk

Chair

Sewing Machine with Filing Cabinets underneath

Built-in Sewing Machine

Chair

Built-in Serger

Cutting Table with Gridded Rotary Mat, Tools and Notions Storage Drawers underneath

Garment Rack

Pressing Table with Pattern Storage Drawers underneath

Printer and Filing Cabinets

Computer Workstation

Chair

Door to Hallway and Residence

Walk-in Fabric Pantry with Shelves

Master Bath Area (layout not shown)

Dream Sewing Spaces

Anita consulted with professional studio designer Lynette Ranney Black on the layout to make sure she hadn't overlooked anything. Lynette helped her plan furniture and equipment placement for optimum work flow, and advised her to add direct task lighting. Lynette is the author of the book featured on this page.

BARBARA WRIGHT SYKES

About The Author

Barbara Wright Sykes is no stranger to success. She has been the host of a popular radio talk show, and the author of *Overcoming Doubt, Fear and Procrastination,* as well as numerous books, audio's, forms and software. Barbara has been a frequent guest on television and radio, making 125 radio appearances in one year alone. Her TV appearances include: KTLA, BET, WGN, ABC, CBS, and Crook and Chase. Ms. Wright Sykes has been recognized and praised by leading newspapers and magazines such as the Los Angeles Times, Chicago Tribune, Income Opportunity, and Health Magazine.

Barbara had been the recipient of the prestigious **"International Woman of the Year"** award for her contribution in the fields of business and psychology. Receiving this honor ranked Barbara Wright Sykes in the company of such notables as former President Reagan's daughter Maureen Regan, noted attorney Gloria Alred, journalist Linda Ellerbee, actress Mariette Hartley, news anchor Kelly Lang, and actress Renee Taylor of *The Nanny* television show.

Serving as a business consultant for professionals desiring to start, maintain and achieve success, Barbara founded the firm Barbara Wright & Associates in 1979. Barbara has consulted with: California State University, Midwestern State University, Union Bank and Vogue Magazine, among others. As a successful sewing professional, Barbara was commissioned by the fashion industries noted designers, tailors and sewing professionals to assist them with pricing, market analysis and business expansion. She penned her first business text book, entitled *The "Business" Of Sewing.* In demand as a business consultant, KTLA's popular morning show "Making It' featured Barbara Wright Sykes as one of Southern California's leading speakers, business consultants and authors.

Stimulating a broad wave of discussion, while arming a vast generation of individuals with the tools necessary for a successful personal and professional life, Barbara travels throughout the year lecturing to standing-room only seminars for corporations, colleges, universities and the private sector. She has served as keynote speaker and workshop facilitator for Wells Fargo Bank, Department of Agriculture, Small Business Development Center, and the International Woman's Council, to name a few.

Barbara has a myriad of knowledge and expertise, she formerly taught college in such disciplines as business, psychology and career development, for which she received the Outstanding Instructor Award. She has developed several popular seminars among those are: *Overcoming Doubt, Fear and Procrastination*; *Pricing Without Fear; Marketing Your Sewing Business; The "Business" Of Sewing; Getting Published—From Concept To Consumer; The Five Layers of Relationships* and her most requested *"Yes I Can."* Barbara inspires people with her down-to-earth wisdom, as she guides individuals to their life-long goals. Her motto, "Determination Equals Success!" encourages individuals to look forward to the personal and spiritual satisfaction that life has to offer.

Barbara Wright Sykes has been appreciated and recognized for her hard work and dedication to others. Those who know her well, speak highly of her: One of Atlanta's most successful businessmen had this to say about Barbara: *"I have learned much by observing Barbara in action. It is impossible to know her without experiencing a wealth of energy and enthusiasm. If you're going someplace in life, you will want to know Barbara Wright Sykes . She is a winner."* — S. Barry Hamdani

To schedule an interview, personal appearance, speaking engagement or consultation with Barbara contact: Ann Collins at Voice: 909-606-1009 or Fax: 909-393-6217

About Collins Publications

Since 1991 Collins Publications has been dedicated to helping you achieve your goals. We have a wide variety of quality products to teach you how to deal with your fears and enhance personal relationships; improve your business, learn computer software, sew for profit, self-publish your books, and even purchase a computer! We also offer consulting on a wide variety of topics. Our number one goal is to provide you with the tools for success, by offering excellent products, outstanding service, and friendly and helpful staff!

Sewing For Profit Forum: For those of you interested in Sewing for Profit, we will be featuring a wealth of information on our web site www.collinspub.com. You will find everything from interviews with the nations leading sewing professionals to tips and articles on how to make your sewing business a success. Make *The Sewing For Profit Forum* your favorite place for new information, and to keep in touch with your colleagues. Send us your questions and one of our advisors will answer it on the internet. List your specialty (bridal, etc.). Join our mailing list and receive sewing for profit updates.

Directory Of Sewing Professional: Because we have sewing for profit on our web site people all over the world ask us where they can find a sewing professional. After numerous inquiries we decided to offer a referral service on our web site. You may place your card or small ad in our directory for a nominal fee. Call 800-795-8999 for more information or send a self-addressed, stamped envelop for more information.

Speaking/ Book Signings/ Library/ Special Appearance/ Press/ Radio, and TV: To book an engagement with one of our authors please call our Public Relations Dept. We will send a fee schedule and availability update. Call 909-606-1009

Wholesale Information: Call, Fax or email your request to Collins Publications, and we will send our wholesale terms and discounts. Call 909-606-1009

Book and Product Submissions: If you have books or products that fit into any one of our four divisions, you may call for our submissions guidelines. Call 909-606-1009 or visit our web site.

Self Publishing: If you have a book you wish to self publish call 909-606-1009 or visit our web site

Free Catalog

We have four divisions at Collins Publications, they are:

■Sewing For Profit   ■Self Publishing   ■Self Help   ■Software Training

Call us for your copy of the latest catalog: 800-795-8999 or 909-606-1009
Or visit or web site at: www.collinspub.com or mail to: ***Collins Publications***
(email: collins@collinspub.com)
3233 Grand Ave., Ste. N-294C
Chino Hills, CA 91709

Start Your Business With Confidence

Overcoming Doubt Fear and Procrastination $24.95 by Barbara Wright Sykes

Two out of three people suffer from doubt, fear and procrastination. Many find that each year they never reach their goals and objectives, ultimately diminishing the quality of their personal and professional lives. This book teaches you principles to help you identify the symptoms associated with doubt, fear and procrastination and overcome the obstacles. You will learn how to develop a sense of urgency. You will acquire a sincere desire to change your attitude and modify negative behavior. You will gain a level of commitment that will allow you to become successful. You will learn to leave your comfort zone and exude confidence and self esteem. Recognized by the *LA Times*, *Health Magazine*, and *Income Opportunity*, noted author, lecturer and consultant, **Barbara Wright Sykes** presents a very powerful and easy approach that is packed with results. *(audio and workbook available)*

Workbook: Overcoming Doubt Fear and Procrastination $9.95 by Barbara Wright Sykes

So many people read books, get pumped up and never follow through. To insure maximum success *Barbara Wright Sykes* developed a tool allowing you to apply the principles outlined in *Overcoming Doubt, Fear and Procrastination*. It's a wonderful companion guide that works in tandem with the book. It will motivate you to accomplish the exercises and principals that insure your desired success in overcoming doubt, fear and procrastination once and for all. Getting what you want out of life doesn't have to be hard. One things for certain, once you commit to paper, you are serious about making a change. The workbook makes it fun and enjoyable. Order now—Do it for "YOU!" See Barbara's column on our website under News/Reviews: Self Help Issue **www.collinspub.com**

Audio: Overcoming Doubt Fear and Procrastination $16.95 by Barbara Wright Sykes

Having a bad hair day? Can't seem to get your motor revved up? Nothing is going right at home or on the job? Did you get out of bed on the wrong side? You need a boost. Listening to Barbara Wright Sykes will infuse your soul with enthusiasm and encourage you to initiate change to make a difference in your life—"Right Now." Her energy is infectious. After listening to Barbara, you'll discover that you have the power to make a difference in your world. You don't have to accept defeat, low self-esteem, lack of confidence, feelings of shame and guilt, poor time management, the need to be a perfectionist or the need to gain approval, acceptance and permission from anyone. Learn the symptoms of doubt, fear and procrastination. What a benefit: You will achieve goals, tasks, projects, resolutions, and conquer time management. Discover how to structure personal and professional relationships that put you in the drivers seat. You can listen 24 hours a day, 7 days a week, 365 days a year!

COLLINS PUBLICATIONS
3233 Grand Ave., Suite N-294C
Chino Hills, CA 91709
Website: www.collinspub.com
Email: collins@collinspub.com

Order Form

Credit Card Orders: (800) 795-8999
Customer service: (909) 590-2471
Fax: (909) 628-9330

VISA   AMERICAN EXPRESS   MasterCard

☐ Regular Shipping ☐ Airmail Shipping

Join The Directory Of Sewing Professionals
Use your coupon and save $2 off shipping
Get a Free Catalog

TITLE	PRICE	QTY	TOTAL

Regular Shipping/Handling (US Funds Only)

Up to $25...............$4.90	$26 to $50.............$6.90	$51 to $100.............$8.90
$101 to $150..........$10.90	$151 to $175.......$12.90	$176 to $199.......$14.90
$200 plus............$16.90	Add $3.00 Canada,	Add $6.00 International

Regular Shipping Takes 3-5 weeks; air-mail takes 3-5 working days: Air Mail: Add $1.95 to S/H for US. Call for Next Day and 2nd Day Air

SUB-TOTAL	
Minus Coupon	
New Sub-Total	

Prices subject to change without notice. Attach separate sheet for additional products.

Tax (8% CA Residents)	
Shipping & Handling	
Total (US Funds Only)	

Name: _____ Date: _____

Company: _____

Home Phone: _____ Fax: _____ E-Mail: _____

Website: _____

Address: _____ City: _____

State: _____ Zip: _____ Payment Method: ☐ Check #_____ ☐ Visa ☐ MasterCard ☐ American Express

Credit Card # : _____ Exp. Date: _____

Name on Card: _____ Signature: _____

❶ ❷ ❸ ❹ ❺ ❻ ❼ ❽

1. Knit A Business: The Knitter's Guide to Starting A Business **$19.95** Includes Learning the Industry; Getting Started; Developing Prototype and Sample Line; Pricing; Marketing; Reps; Manufacturing; Production/Financial Planning; Using Home knitters; Shipping/Receiving/Customer Service; Time Management & more. *by Jane Ambrose Button*

2. Sew A Business: Guide to Starting A Clothing Business or Sewn Product Company **$19.95** Includes chapters on: Getting Started; Getting Your Product Ready for Market; Creating A Prototype; Developing A Sample Line; Pricing; Marketing Strategies; All You Need to Know About Sales Reps; Manufacturing; Production Planning; Using Home workers; Shipping & Receiving; Customer Service; Financial Planning and Time Management for Creative People! And more. *by Jane Ambrose Button (She's featured in Pricing Without Fear)*

3. Creative Sewing As A Business $15.95 Turn your creative ideas into cash selling to galleries, gift shops, boutiques, art fairs, and trade shows, as well as, writing, teaching, and designing. Includes easy to use business forms/record keeping systems. Learn how to market, find suppliers and buy wholesale. You'll achieve your goals, increase sales and build a successful business. Saundra Weed is featured in *Pricing Without Fear. by Saundra Weed*

4. Bridal Couture $29.95 Learn major techniques used to sew couture creations: choosing fabrics, working with lace, creating a muslin, solving difficult construction issues. All styles of skirt, sleeve, and bodice is included with fabric suggestions. Details of four actual gowns, give readers a chance to apply what they've learned. Susan Khalje's a writer for *Threads Magazine* and is featured in *Pricing Without Fear. by Susan Khalje*

5. Dream Sewing Spaces $19.95 Turn your dreams into a reality and get inspiration from gorgeous color photos, diagrams and helpful hints will provide inspiration for a wide variety of sewing spaces. Learn how to build and where to buy furniture. The studio Anita Greene is featured in was designed by the author of this book. (see picture above) *by Lynette Rainey Black*

6. Forms for Custom Interiors/Home Décor $49.00 38 forms for interior designers, sewing workrooms, and fabricator trade professionals. Included are business organization forms, client record keeping spread sheets, estimation worksheets, measurement and design forms, work orders and more! Trenia Bell-Will has designed for McCall's Pattern Company and is featured in *Pricing Without Fear. byTrenia Bell-Will*

7. Sew To Success $10.95 Kathleen Spike, founder of *Professional Association Of Custom Clothiers* and writer for *Sew News* magazine, shares her knowledge and expertise on how to achieve success in a home based sewing business. Included are pricing methods, resources and much more.

8. Patterns by La Fred: Call **1-800-795-8999** for a free catalog or visit or web site **www.collinspub.com.**